CW00535941

THE YORKSHIRE DALES
THE NORTH AND EAST

About the authors

Both native Lancastrians, Dennis and Jan Kelsall have long held a passion for countryside and hill walking. Since their first Cicerone title was published in 1995, they have written and illustrated around 45 guides covering some of Britain's most popular walking areas and regularly contribute to various outdoor magazines. Their enjoyment of the countryside extends far beyond a love of fresh air, the freedom of open spaces and an appreciation of scenery. Over the years Dennis and Jan have developed a wide interest in the environment, its geology and wildlife, as well as an enthusiasm for delving into the local history that so often provides clues to interpreting the landscape.

Their other Cicerone titles explore the coast and countryside of Pembrokeshire, the Ribble Way, the variety of landscapes along the River Lune and its tributaries and the companion volume to this guide covering the southern and western areas of the Yorkshire Dales.

Other Cicerone guidebooks by the authors
The Pembrokeshire Coastal Path
The Ribble Way
The Yorkshire Dales: South and West
Walking in Pembrokeshire

THE YORKSHIRE DALES
THE NORTH AND EAST
THE HOWGILL FELLS, MALLERSTANG, SWALEDALE, WENSLEYDALE, COVERDALE AND NIDDERDALE

by

Dennis and Jan Kelsall

JUNIPER HOUSE, MURLEY MOSS,
OXENHOLME ROAD, KENDAL, CUMBRIA LA9 7RL
www.cicerone.co.uk

© Dennis and Jan Kelsall 2015
Second edition 2015
ISBN 978 1 85284 798 2
Reprinted 2018 and 2020 (with updates)
First edition 2009

Printed in China on responsibly sourced paper on behalf of Latitude Press Ltd
A catalogue record for this book is available from the British Library.
All photographs are by the authors unless otherwise stated.

Updates to this Guide

While every effort is made by our authors to ensure the accuracy of guide-books as they go to print, changes can occur during the lifetime of an edition. Any updates that we know of for this guide will be on the Cicerone website (www.cicerone.co.uk/798/updates), so please check before planning your trip. We also advise that you check information about such things as transport, accommodation and shops locally. Even rights of way can be altered over time. We are always grateful for information about any discrepancies between a guidebook and the facts on the ground, sent by email to updates@cicerone.co.uk or by post to Cicerone, Juniper House, Murley Moss, Oxenholme Road, Kendal LA9 7RL United Kingdom.

Register your book: To sign up to receive free updates, special offers and GPX files where available, register your book at www.cicerone.co.uk.

Front cover: *The Nab above Mallerstang Gorge (Walk 12)*

CONTENTS

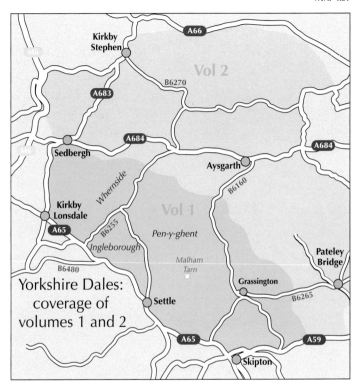

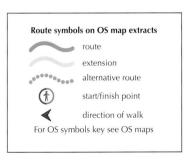

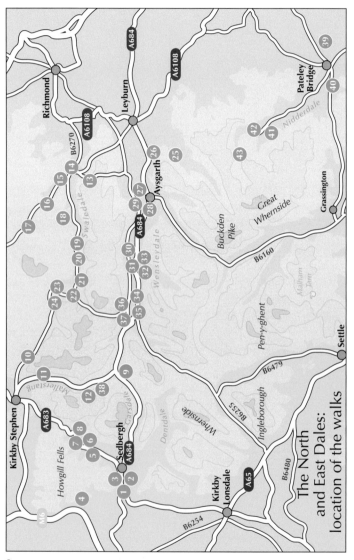

The North and East Dales: location of the walks

INTRODUCTION

Looking beyond Keld to distant Lovely Seat (Walk 24)

THE DALES LANDSCAPE

The Yorkshire Dales is like nowhere else in England, a place of intrinsic and striking beauty that owes its scenic qualities both to nature and to man. Bestriding the central Pennines, that broad range of hills erupting along the middle of the country, and known to generations of schoolchildren as the 'backbone of England', the Dales boasts a diversity of landscape and character that is hard to beat.

Walkers trudging up the Pennine Way from the south into Craven leave the sombre mill valleys that fragment the desolate, weather-beaten moors of West Yorkshire and East Lancashire to be greeted by a brighter, more intimate scene of interwoven horizons. Rolling green hills, broken here and there by rugged scars of white limestone, rise to a distant, higher ground dissected by deepening valleys. Further east and to the north, the wild moors dominate, but even here a varied geology of underlying rock breaks up their melancholic uniformity.

It is perhaps perverse that, as an upland region, the Yorkshire Dales is named after its most low-lying elements. But, like the neighbouring Lake District, it is this complementary feature that determines its endearing uniqueness. Just as the Cumbrian mountains would be the less without scintillating tarns and lakes to reflect

9

Field barns are a feature of the Wensleydale pastures (Walk 30)

their awesome ruggedness, the character of the Dales hills relies on the gentle beauty that rises up from the long, deep and twisting valleys emanating from the core. Devoid of the dramatic impact of soaring peaks, knife-edge ridges and great hanging valleys, the mountains here might otherwise be regarded as unremarkable, with little to distinguish them from the other hills of the Pennine range, but their intimacy with the gentle valleys that they enclose is what truly sets them apart.

Despite the steep gradients that act as boundaries between the upper moors and the lowlands, it is often hard to define where the one begins and the other ends. Stroll in rich water meadows beside a serpentine river flowing in a flat-bottomed valley, or stride upon an airy plateau beneath vast, open skies, and there is little doubt where you are. But walk from one to the other and the transition is often quite subtle. In many places, the neatly walled grazing pastures of the lower valleys climb high up the slope, sometimes intermingled with variegated woodlands that soften the craggy steps. In their higher reaches, the valley bottoms can often feel utterly remote from the rest of the world, and have an untamed complexion that is more akin to the uplands. On the wildest of the tops, great morasses of peat hag and bog might stretch for miles, but even here the tendrils of the ubiquitous stone walls are never

far away, encompassing bleak tracts of land and signifying a belonging to some farm settlement in the valley far below.

Ancient trackways and paths ignore these geographical divisions, and connect this dale to that, or lead up to small mines and quarries that were often as integral to a farming income as the cows' milk and ewes' wool. Although the contours of the land mean that summits are rarely visible from the valley floor, and vice versa, for much of the way in between, the wider views encompass them both. And it is from this perspective that the two really do come together to be appreciated as a single entity – the Yorkshire Dales.

Set between the Stainmoor and Aire gaps north and south, the Lune Valley in the west, and running out onto the great expanse of the Vale of York to the east, the Dales covers a relatively compact area of upland plateau fragmented by a number of main valley systems. The tumbling rivers of the Swale, Ure, Nidd, Wharfe and Aire all unite in the River Ouse, which, meeting the Trent, becomes the Humber as it runs into the North Sea. The Ribble, together with those streams gathered by the peripheral Lune, finds its freedom to the west in the Irish Sea, while Mallerstang alone drains northward along the Eden Valley to Carlisle and the Solway Firth. Feeding these main rivers is a multitude of lesser ones that gnaw deep into the heartland, creating a maze of smaller valleys and

West Close Barn in Sleddale (Walk 34)

dales, each proclaiming its own subtly different character.

This variance is rooted in underlying geology and positional geography, and is also the product of elemental forces, but important too is the way man has settled and exploited the Dales over millennia. Farming, husbandry, woodland management, quarrying and mining have all left their mark on the slopes, and here, at least, it can be said that the cumulative efforts of successive generations has unconsciously helped in the creation of one of the loveliest landscapes in the country.

Although numerous lanes and tracks wind deep into the heart of the Dales, it is really only the leisurely freedom of pedestrian exploration

that enables a true appreciation of its unique charm. This, the second of two volumes, is a wanderer's guide to the northern and eastern parts of the area, savouring its ups, downs and endless in-betweens. The various walks seek out spectacular viewpoints, dramatic landforms, curious natural features and attractive hamlets and villages, but more than that, they simply delight in the subtly changing scenery. There is something for everyone in this guidebook, from gentle walks along valleys and hillsides, to more demanding upland romps that take in the high hills and remote moors of the hinterland. For the newcomer in particular, this is an invaluable companion. In addition to the route descriptions, there is background information on many of the features encountered along the way. While some routes are inevitably popular, many others take you off the beaten track to less-visited spots, and even those who know the Dales may well find new corners.

EVOLUTION OF THE LANDSCAPE

Geological history

The unique character and unquestionable charm of the Yorkshire Dales has its roots in the underlying bedrock, much of which was created during the Carboniferous period 300 million years ago. At a time when, in other areas, massive coal, gas and oil fields were being laid down in the accumulating detritus of humid forest swamps, the area which has become the Dales lay beneath a shallow tropical sea. Here, the broken shells of countless marine creatures settled to form a bed of limestone over 200m thick. Known as the Great Scar Limestone, it dominates the scenery of the southwestern corner of the Yorkshire Dales National Park and underlies its central core.

Eventually, river deltas encroached from the north, washing mud and sand across the coastal shelf. But this was a period of cyclically changing sea levels, creating sequential strata of shale and weak sandstones, repeatedly topped off by limestone as lagoon conditions intermittently returned. Each band is only around 12m thick, but the build up over aeons formed a kind of 'layer cake', over 300m deep.

The River Ure at Slapestone Wath (Walk 28)

Named the Yoredale Series, because of its appearance in the valley of the River Ure – Wensleydale – this banded rock forms the basis of the northern portion of the national park, and extends further south as higher peaks and ridges. The upper levels of the layering culminate in a hard, impervious sandstone known as millstone grit, reflecting one of its uses, and the remnants of this form the southern hill tops and the high ground of the northern fells.

Although originally laid down in neat, horizontal bands, these rocks were subsequently folded by a massive earth movement that created the Pennines. Fractures separated the section underlying the Yorkshire Dales, known as the Askrigg Block, from the rest of the mountain chain, and it was pushed up from the south and the west, putting the Carboniferous strata of the block far above the younger rocks that lie to the south. The block tilts gently backwards, and whereas weathering has exposed the older limestones in the southwest of the area, the more recent Yoredale rocks remain on top to the northeast.

The lines of fracture are dramatically evident in the three main Craven Faults, which cut across the southern part of the national park. Giggleswick Scar – the line of towering cliffs overlooking the B6480 west of Settle – is part of the South Craven Fault, which continues its line southeast towards Skipton. The Mid-Craven Fault is marked by a long line of cliffs of which

Malham Cove and Gordale Scar are a part, while the North Craven Fault runs parallel to it at the southern lip of Malham Tarn.

In a few places, the limestone of the block has been worn away to expose rocks from an even earlier era, the Ordovician, which, unlike the even Carboniferous formations, are extravagantly crumpled, and consist of slates, grits and mudstones. These can be seen in the quarries of Ribblesdale and around Ingleton, and are also exposed as an impervious basement layer in the southern valleys, perhaps most vividly in Thornton Force and along the Ingleton Falls.

The character of the Howgills clearly sets them apart from the rest of the Dales, and with the Middleton Fells, they are separated from the Askrigg Block by another fracture line – the Dent Fault. This runs in a rough north–south line east of Sedbergh, but here the displacement has been in the opposite direction, elevating the older rocks that lie to the west. Geologically these hills are part of the Lake District, and are composed of much-folded metamorphosed slates and grits from the Silurian period, about 100 million years older than the Carboniferous rocks making up the Askrigg Block. Their grassy flanks sweep steeply upwards from deep ravines to broad, rounded tops, whose long interconnecting ridges, once attained, offer immensely satisfying walking.

Some of the most spectacular scenery of the national park is to be

Field barn above the River Swale below Ivelet Side (Walk 21)

found in the areas dominated by the Great Scar Limestone – Malham Cove, Gordale, Kingsdale, Twisleton, Lower Ribblesdale and the middle reaches of Wharfedale. Towering lines of white cliffs and scars, shake holes, sinks, potholes, caves, disappearing and resurgent streams and rivers, dry valleys and waterfalls, clints and grikes, are all features of this remarkable karst landscape. Overlooking the fault lines, the cliffs result from the upward movement of the Askrigg Block, but the terraces along the valley side are due to the relative resistance of different layers to erosive weathering. A similar picture is seen further north in the Yoredale Series, where the successive bands of limestone are comparatively harder than the intervening strata of sandstones, producing the

stepped profile that is so characteristic of Wharfedale and Swaledale. It is this same process that gives rise to the many spectacular waterfalls of the region, the water cascading over a lip of hard limestone, but undercutting into the softer rock that lies below.

The most intriguing features of karst landscapes are those that result from the solubility of the bedrock in rainwater. The rain's slight acidity dissolves the stone, exploiting crevices and vertical stress fractures, and ultimately creating the awe-inspiring potholes and caves for which the area is famous. Whole rivers are swallowed into the ground, either in abruptly sensational falls such as Gaping Gill, or merely disappearing intermittently into their beds, as does the River Nidd in its higher reaches.

15

Just as magical are the Nidd's resurgences lower down, the river having coursed between two points deep underground in the dark and constricted passages and fissures that are the province of intrepid potholers and cave divers. At Stump Cross, these dramatic passages are sufficiently accessible to have been opened as show caves, allowing visitors to marvel at fantastic stalactites, stalagmites and other formations, created as incessant drips of lime-rich water evaporated over millennia, leaving the lime behind. Occasionally, similar deposits are also seen on the surface in the form of tufa, where calcite is precipitated from the cascading water. And at How Stean Gorge, the river runs through a dramatically narrow canyon, which is explained as a collapsed cave.

While streams, even after rain, are something of a rarity on the limestone uplands of the south, dry valleys are not. Like Trow Gill and Conistone Dib, they can be stunningly spectacular – deep, narrow ravines, stepped with the walls of ancient waterfalls. Occasionally, following heavy rain, rivulets might briefly cascade through, but these bear little resemblance to the overwhelming torrents of meltwater that created them, as the last ice age came to an end. Where rivers flow uninterrupted today, they have usually worn the valley down to a bedrock of impervious stone, or else flow over deposits of clay dumped by retreating glaciers.

16

The extensive clint fields, or limestone pavements, also have their origins in the last ice age. Initially levelled to a bedding plane and stripped clean by glacial action, they were re-covered with clay debris when the ice finally retreated. Seeping rainwater subsequently picked out vertical lines of weakness to form the grikes, fragmenting the pavement into blocks – the clints. Eventual erosion of the thin soil cover, perhaps as a result of woodland clearance, or grazing by early man's livestock, has once more revealed the bare pavements that are now such a striking feature. Accumulating soil in the base of the grikes holds moisture, and this shelter creates micro-habitats that are home to an astonishing variety of plantlife, rare on an otherwise quite barren landscape.

Also composed of limestone, although of a different formation to the Great Scar, is a striking line of small hills between Malham and Grassington. Termed reef knolls, they are the remnants of a coral barrier reef that marked the edge of a shelf in the shallow sea. Erosion of the later, overlying softer deposits has revealed these submarine hillocks once more, distinctive because of their conical shape.

Away from the Great Scar, the scenery is no less stirring – a great plateau of high ground fragmented by deep valleys, with just a few mountain tops daring to poke their flat heads above the rest. Most famous amongst these are the Yorkshire Three Peaks

Looking across the foot of Arkengarthdale to Calver Hill (Walk 15)

– Whernside, Ingleborough and Pen-y-ghent – planted well apart around the head of Ribblesdale. But the northern part of the Dales boasts its own heights in Baugh Fell, Wild Boar Fell, Great Shunner Fell and others.

Although not one of the Dales peaks culminates in a dramatic pinnacle summit, their flanks climb steeply out of the surrounding valleys, rising in terraces through the Yoredale Series. Alternating bands of springy grass and lines of sink holes, heather heath and then marsh, reflect the nature of the changing geology underfoot, culminating in an undulating upland bog held upon the upper sandstone and gritstone cap.

It is this layering too that is responsible for the impressive waterfalls in Wensleydale, in particular the falls on the River Ure at Aysgarth, and the great cascade of Hardraw Force above Hawes. Shake holes too are a common feature of the bands of limestone, and nowhere are they more spectacular than beside the Buttertubs Pass.

While geology and subterranean force may have laid the foundation for the Dales landscape, it is the natural elements that have been responsible for moulding it. And nothing has been more dramatic in its effect than the action of ice. During the last half-million years of its history, Britain has been subjected to at least three major ice ages, when vast glacial sheets, many hundreds of feet thick, inexorably fanned out from the mountain areas across much of the country. Although the general topography of the area had already been set before

17

Old miners' cottages in Langthwaite (Walk 16)

the ice ages began, each new advance scoured the land back to the very bedrock, gouging valleys ever deeper, and straightening their erratic fluvial courses. When the thaws came, boulder and clay debris were dumped far from their origins, and unimaginable volumes of water were released. What we see today are just the finishing touches left by the latest glacial period, whose icy tendrils melted from these valleys 12,000 years ago.

The legacy of the ice can been traced throughout the Dales in characteristic rounded hills, straight U-shaped valleys and the dramatic cliffs of truncated spurs. The moving ice carried boulders long distances, and moulded underlying clay into distinctive egg-shaped hills called drumlins, which can be seen to fine advantage in Wensleydale and Ribblesdale. With the thaw, the unstable sides of overly steep valleys slumped in landslide, and layers of boulder clay were dumped along the base of valleys, allowing surface rivers to flow over limestone.

Some dales were dammed with terminal moraines that held back lakes, but all but two of these – Malham Tarn and Semer Water – have subsequently silted up or drained away. The deluge of meltwater cut spectacularly narrow ravines through the rock and created majestic waterfalls. Some of these still carry water today – although mere trickles by comparison with the former torrents of their creation – and are well worth looking out for.

Human settlement

Homo sapiens appeared in Europe some 40,000 years ago, and during the warm interludes between glaciation, wandered into Britain. But with each ice age driving them back south and wiping the archaeological slate almost clean, those early incursions of people, and the beasts that they followed for food, have left few traces.

Stone Age peoples eventually returned to the Dales around 9000 years ago, small bands of hunter-gatherers eking a nomadic existence in a steadily warming climate. Although artefacts are thin on the ground, they left their mark by beginning the clearance of primeval woodland, a process that gathered momentum with the later development of agriculture and the transition to a more settled lifestyle. The many caves and crevices in the limestone hills served as shelters for living and burial, a fact which perhaps explains the relative absence here of the constructed internment chambers, cairns and henges found elsewhere in the country.

By the time of the Bronze Age, large areas had been cleared for grazing and agriculture, but a deterioration in climate led to the spread of extensive blanket bog across the upper plateaux.

While habitation sites and field systems from earlier eras are known, their more prominent traces have been largely obliterated by later settlement, and there is little visible evidence pre-dating the Iron Age.

Collapsed stone walls line the processional entrance to Maiden Castle (Walk 14)

The area fell within the territory of a British tribe known as the Brigantes, and many settlement sites and earthwork structures have been identified. Maiden Castle above Reeth and the extensive fortification surrounding the summit of Ingleborough are amongst the most spectacular examples.

Although the Romans did establish a permanent fort at Bainbridge around AD80, they never really subjugated the hill tribes. In fact there appears to have been a relatively peaceful co-existence with lowland farmers, who would have found ready markets for their produce in the Roman economy until the eventual withdrawal of the occupation forces a little over three centuries later. The enigmatic patterns of those small Celtic fields still survive in several places, most notably above Malham and Grassington.

The early years of the seventh century saw the arrival of Angle settlers, who continued a tradition of arable farming along the dales, reserving the higher, less productive ground of the valley sides for woodland and grazing. The lynchets (ridges) of their open field systems, created by ploughing with teams of oxen along the slopes of the valley sides, survived through the medieval period, and are still visible above Malham and around Clapham and Reeth. The process of sporadic settlement continued throughout the Dark Ages, as successive waves of immigration brought the Vikings, their presence reflected in place names such as Yokenthwaite, Hawkswick,

Appletreewick, and indeed the word 'dale' itself.

The next millennium heralded the new age of the invading Normans. After he had won the day, William the Conqueror consolidated his position by beating the northern part of his kingdom into submission with a heavy and cruel hand. The overlords ruled from peripheral fortress towns such as Skipton, Richmond and Barnard Castle, exploiting the remoter reaches of the Dales as hunting forests, and establishing markets that thrived serving the larger centres of population.

During the succeeding centuries, much of the region was gradually encompassed within vast monastic estates. Fountains Abbey and the priory at Bolton Abbey became the greatest landowners, but houses such

as Furness on the Cumbrian coast and Bridlington far to the east also held significant tracts of land here. Under the careful administration and watchful eyes of the abbots and priors, the farms made their money from wool, as well as growing a range of staple crops. The monasteries also exploited the mineral resources of the region, mining for coal, lead and other metals.

After the Dissolution of the Monasteries in the 16th century, ownership of much of the land eventually fell to individual freeholding farmers. By the 17th century, agricultural improvements and an expanding lead industry began to engender a climate of growing personal prosperity, and brought with it a new confidence that was translated into

From the ruin of the Quaker Meeting House to the burial ground at East Scale (Walk 9)

building in stone. It is from this era that the earliest domestic buildings survive, sturdily constructed from rough stone, with dressed blocks being reserved for corners, lintels and window openings. They reflect the local geology, in limestone, gritstone, and heavy stone flags for the roofs. Although largely utilitarian and lacking ornate decoration, individualism is nevertheless displayed in the carvings of dates and initials on lintels above doorways.

Grouped in compact villages, often overlooking a green, or spread as individual farms along the valley, they are one of the endearing features of the Dales countryside. Long and narrow, the farmhouses often included an attached barn – or laithe – for the animals, and in some areas, notably Swaledale and Wensleydale, isolated barns were built in the valley fields to store summer hay and house livestock over winter.

Industry and enterprise

The relative inaccessibility of the region protected it from the burgeoning development of the Industrial Revolution, for, even though it held abundant raw materials in stone, coal and metal ore, the difficulties of transportation often rendered large-scale growth uneconomic. Yet, despite its comparatively small scale, mining and quarrying did become important local money-making activities, sometimes worked on a part-time basis to supplement income

from farming. The abandoned ruins of pit-head buildings, smelters and disused quarries are to be found scattered throughout the region, often in the most inhospitable of places.

Veins of lead ore occur in the limestone throughout the eastern and northern parts of the Dales, and have been mined sporadically since the arrival of the Romans. Following the Industrial Revolution, the industry peaked during the middle 18th and early 19th centuries, but then fell into decline because of high transport costs, competition from foreign imports, and the simple fact that many seams had been worked to their economic limit. Nevertheless, over the centuries huge amounts were produced, and it has been estimated that over half a million tonnes of metallic lead have been excavated from Swaledale alone, with more than half of this coming solely from the Old Gang mines above Surrender Bridge.

Where there is lead, there is often silver too, albeit it small amounts, and the Duke of Devonshire's Cupola Mine above Grassington produced a significant amount of silver as a by-product before it closed in 1885. In the area further west, around Malham, copper and zinc ores were also discovered, and more recently deposits of baryte and fluorspar have been worked in the Dales.

Such enterprise brought with it a dramatic increase in population, attracting miners and ordinary

Old Gang mill (Walk 18)

labourers from across the country. Some came on their own, but others brought their families too, expanding the tiny villages. In Muker, for example, the new part of the village by the main lane is quite distinct from the old heart, and in many villages you will find chapels, village halls and reading rooms that all resulted from this boom. Inevitably, as the lead industry declined, the population drifted away, some heading northeast to continue their trade in the coal mines, while others went to try their hand in the textile valleys of Lancashire and west Yorkshire.

To the north and on the high ground, the Yoredale rocks contain thin seams of coal of varying quality. These were intermittently mined from the beginning of the 14th century until the railway age, often from small workings called bell pits. The coal supplied domestic needs as well as being used on a larger scale to fire smelt furnaces and lime kilns. On the bleak top of Fountains Fell, coal was even processed in an oven to produce coke, a trouble worth taking to reduce the weight of the product to be carried down the hill. Another important source of fuel both for the home and the mines was peat, cut from turbaries (places where turf or peat is dug) on the upland bogs.

All these activities have long since finished, but not so the extensive stone quarries around Horton in Ribblesdale and at Linton, which serve the chemical industry and provide aggregate for building, roads and railways. Sadly, these massive workings are a scar on the landscape, a far cry from the earlier, small-scale operations that produced stone for local building and walling, and to produce lime fertiliser. At first glance, these old, abandoned workings are now barely distinguishable from their natural backdrop, something their modern-day equivalents might find harder to achieve once they have been worked out.

Any other enterprise that developed was only ever on a limited scale. Fast-flowing streams in the main valleys powered grist and, later, other mills, with textiles becoming significant in some corners, such as Grassington and Aysgarth. Just as important was the widespread cottage textile industry, carried out in individual farms and cottages, not least to the northwest, where gloves and stockings fell off clattering needles, wielded by woman, child and man alike, in such prodigious quantities that these people become known as 'the terrible knitters of Dent'.

The major inhibiting factor for industry was a lack of suitable transport to main industrial centres. Turnpikes through the Dales were few, and the canal age touched only the southern portals at Gargrave and Skipton. The engineering determination of the Victorians served them better, as the entrepreneurial spirit pushed the railways deep into the heart of the region, along Wensleydale and into Wharfedale.

Ambitious plans conceived for links into the lesser valleys never came to fruition, although a crowning achievement was realised in 1876 in the Settle–Carlisle line. It was forced through by the Midland Railway at great financial and human cost, ironically not to serve the Dales but to compete with existing mainline routes to Scotland. For a while, the railway sustained trade along the western fringes and into Wensleydale, enabling rapid transportation of dairy products to satisfy the markets of industrial towns. But the boom was short-lived, and now only a mineral railway track and the famous Settle–Carlisle line remain, and the latter's future was only secured in 1989, at the end of a long and hard-fought battle after it was threatened with closure in the 1980s.

But, while railways and main roads are few, innumerable paths and tracks criss-cross the whole area. Some may have their origins in pre-historic times, others, like the Cam High Road above Bainbridge, follow the lines of Roman roads, while many more were trodden by the monks and lay workers of the great medieval abbeys and priories as they administered their far-flung estates.

Dating from pre-industrial Britain, pack-horse trails and cattle drove roads were once the main arteries of trade, while other tracks connected small settlements to market towns. Some of the tracks that appear on today's maps now appear rather pointless, ending abruptly on the slope of a bare hillside or winding onto the moors to finish in a barren wilderness.

The miners' bridge across Old Gang Beck (Walk 18)

But follow them on the ground and you will come across abandoned turbaries or disused mine and quarry workings. Other tracks, called coffin roads, served a more sombre purpose. Even if a chapel existed in an upper valley, burial rights were generally reserved to the parish churches down below, and so the dead had to be brought down for interment, as was the case in Swaledale. Indeed, there are hardly any routes you can follow in the Dales that do not have some story to tell.

Farming in the Dales

The beauty of the Dales landscape is the product of its history, and it is one of those few places where human influence can be said to have improved upon nature, albeit unintentionally. Even the ravages left by historic mining and quarrying have faded, and the grassed-over spoil heaps, collapsed hollows and moss-grown ruined buildings have now assumed an almost natural quality.

Working life in the Dales seems to have evolved largely in accord with its environment, to create a balance that could be sustained through the passing seasons and from year to year. For example, primeval forest was originally cleared for crops and grazing, but some woodland was always retained to provide fuel and timber. And although the bare upland fells eventually returned to little more than rough grazing, they freed lower land for arable farming and the production of hay.

By and large, the farming here has always been relatively unintensive, working within the limits of the generally poor-quality land and traditional boundaries. Getting on for 5500 miles (8851km) of stone walls divide the valleys into a mosaic of small fields, and fan out up the steep hillsides to define far-reaching territories that meet along the watersheds on the high moorlands above. The walls are everywhere, except around Dentdale, where hedges prevail, and on the Howgills, where boundaries are few.

Although some walls only date back a couple of hundred years to the Enclosure Acts, a few are truly ancient, and hark back to the time of the first tentative farmers. Together with the tidy villages, compact farmsteads, isolated field barns and sporadic lime kilns, they create a built environment that has a visual harmony completely at one with its setting.

But nothing remains static, not even in a farming landscape, and change is inevitable to meet ever-evolving demands. Arable farming disappeared with the arrival of the railways in the latter part of the 19th century, when fresh food could easily be 'imported' from the more productive market garden areas of the country. Dairy farming, beef-cattle and sheep rearing are now the main activities, cattle predominant on the lower farms, with sheep ubiquitous elsewhere.

Indeed, so much do they reflect the character of life in the Dales that the Swaledale sheep has been adopted

Out to check the sheep on Grisedale Common (Walk 9)

as the emblem of the national park. It is only such hardy breeds, with thick, dense fleeces, that are able to survive the harsh conditions and poor grazing of the upper fells, and they are generally only brought down for lambing and shearing, or when deep winter snow blankets the sparse vegetation upon which they otherwise manage to survive.

Although wool was once an important element of the local economy, that of the hill sheep is now used only for carpet manufacture, and low prices often mean that its value is less than the cost of shearing. The lambs are generally sold on to lowland farms for fattening, with the strong ewes being valued as breeding stock. On the moors, the sheep are 'heafed' or 'hefted' to the land, an instinct that keeps them within their own territory. The ewes somehow pass this instinct on to their lambs, which makes the job of the farmer immeasurably easier when it comes to rounding up the flock.

The number of sheep is determined by what the grazing can sustain. Too small and the land will become overrun with scrub, but too much will kill off the heather and denude the grass slopes. Maintaining that delicate balance over the centuries has created the open aspect of the countryside that we so value today.

Long before Wallace and his indefatigable companion, Grommit, revealed their attachment to Wensleydale cheese, dairy farming in the lower dales had been an important

Amongst the cottongrass on the slopes of Dodd Fell Hill (Walk 35)

element in the local economy. Before the arrival of the railway, milk itself could only be used to supply local demand, but the coming of the railway meant that cheese and butter made on farms could be 'exported' for sale in distant towns, even as far away as London. Cheese is still produced in a small factory at Hawes, and although the milk trains no longer run, road tankers make the daily round of farms to supply the bottling and processing plants.

Higher up the valley, the pastures are not as rich, and cattle are bred for meat, being sold on for fattening before finally going to the butcher. Traditionally cattle were sent out to graze riverside meadows in spring before being moved onto higher pastures. During summer, the meadows were left to produce hay, the herd being brought back after the harvest to graze the late growth. Individual field barns – or laithes – removed the need to cart the hay, and meant that cattle could over-winter in the fields rather than be brought back to the farm.

Managing the meadows in this way allowed them to develop a rich herbage of spring and summer flowers, which in turn encouraged a diversity of both insects and birds. In some areas, particularly Swaledale, they are still a delight to behold, but such practices do not sit well alongside pressures to improve productivity. Reseeding and the use of fertilisers and herbicides might double the yield of grass, but the wild flowers that once grew there all but disappear within a season. Many farmers are trying to redress the balance between efficiency and environmental conservation, but the overriding concern must still be a need to earn an income.

PLANTS AND WILDLIFE

Despite human influences, the environment of the Dales supports a great diversity of habitats, whose individual characteristics are broadly governed by altitude and underlying geology.

Much of the upland is underlain by grits and other impervious rocks, and covered by wet blanket bog, where grass, sphagnum and purple moor grass pervade, with heather, bilberry and heath rush dominating where the ground is drier. Many of the better-drained upland heaths are actively managed as grouse moors, where the old growth of heather is periodically burnt off to encourage young shoots. The moors are perhaps at their most attractive during late summer, when the heather blazes in a rich swathe of purple. The limestone grasslands on the other hand are best in spring, when an amazing variety of small flowers, such as buttercup, vetch, rock rose, cranesbill and campion, speckle colour across the landscape. Small patches of woodland are also most appealing in springtime, when bluebells, ramsons and wood anemones abound.

While the limestone pavements themselves are almost devoid of vegetation, the deeper clefts between the clints offer soil, moisture and protection from grazing. Ferns are amongst the most common plants here, but very occasionally a hawthorn might just escape the attentions of sheep and reach maturity. On the floors of the dales, unimproved hay meadows contain a rich mixture of grasses, as well as an abundance of flowers, and are at their best around June. And even if you do not venture off the lanes, you will be charmed by the mass of flowers that sprout from the crevices of walls and underneath hedgerows.

Such an abundance of flowers supports many insects, of which butterflies and moths are most likely to attract attention. The relatively cool climate of the uplands precludes an abundance of species, but amongst those commonly seen are tortoiseshell, peacock, green-veined white, common blue and green hairstreak.

Birds are the most obvious wildlife throughout the dales, and even the most unobservant birdwatcher cannot help noticing them from the highest fells to the depths of the vales. Red grouse, golden plover and curlew are common across the moors, with merlin and even peregrines hunting for food. Skylarks hover high above the upland pastures, and lapwing, snipe and fieldfare are all to be found. The woodlands, too, harbour many small songbirds, and you will often hear – if not actually spot – a woodpecker.

Streams and rivers attract dippers and wagtails as well as sandpipers and oystercatchers.

Apart from the rabbit, which seems to appear just about everywhere where there is grass, and the grey squirrel, which is earning for itself an increasingly bad press, other mammals are more timid and less easy to spot, although, be assured, they are very much present. Roe deer, hare, fox and badger are amongst the larger animals likely to be encountered, and occasionally the native red squirrel might be seen in woodland. The woodmouse, vole and mole are common but shy, and there are several species of bat, which are most in evidence at dusk. Frogs, toads, lizards and even adders also live in the national park.

With such a tremendous variety of landscape within a relatively small area, the Dales offers some of the most satisfying walking to be had in the whole of the country. Its thousands of miles of pathways, tracks and quiet lanes offer endless possibilities for personal exploration, whether it be in gentle riverside strolls or demanding upland treks. The area is criss-crossed by several long-distance trails, such as the Pennine Way and the Coast to Coast, and is also home to the Yorkshire 'Three Peaks Challenge', the 23-mile (37km) ascent of Pen-y-ghent, Whernside and Ingleborough completed in less than 12 hours. But equally, the charming villages and hamlets strung along the valley

Rebuilding a drystone wall (Walk 33)

bottoms make ideal bases for both short and full-day walks. There are also many opportunities to combine a walk with a visit to one of the local attractions, such as the Wensleydale Dairy at Hawes or the museum at Reeth, or perhaps the spectacular show cave at Stump Cross, but the greatest appeal for many who come here is undoubtedly the intrinsic natural beauty of the countryside.

THE NORTHERN AND EASTERN DALES

This volume covers the northern corners of the Dales: the Howgills, Mallerstang, and the catchments of the rivers Swale, Ure and Nidd, the three coming together in the Vale of York as tributaries of Yorkshire's greatest river, the Ouse. The Howgill Fells apart, the overall character of the area is determined by the Yoredale Series of rocks, whose layered strata of limestones, shales and sandstones foster an immense variety in both the wider topography and the diversity of vegetation. In traversing the valley sides, the different rocks and soil are reflected in the flowers, woodland and blanket bogs, as well as in the features of the landscape – outcropping scars, waterfalls, ravine-like valleys and shake holes and caves.

Mallerstang is the only valley oriented to the north, and although intimately connected in both geography and character to the Dales, like part of the Howgill Fells and Nidderdale,

lies outside the national park boundary. This straight, drawn-out valley guides the infant River Eden from its source high on Lunds Fell, hardly a stone's thrown from that of the River Ure, which runs off in completely the opposite direction. The long line of hills on either flank offers splendid, if energetic, ridge walking, and although the base of the valley is traversed by both railway and road, it engenders a distinct feeling of remoteness. Apart from The Moorcock, which in any case lies over the watershed at the head of Wensleydale, it has no pub, and as far down as Nateby, just outside Kirkby Stephen, the only habitation to be found is in a scattering of small farmsteads.

That same rugged beauty and sense of isolation is shared by the upper reaches of Swaledale, whose tributary valleys splay out to probe the bare moorland openness of the Pennines. Lower down, a string of tiny villages all trace their origins to the wave of Norse settlement in the ninth and tenth centuries, interspersed with an almost continuous string of farmsteads. The flanking hillsides are richly veined with seams of lead ore, some of which were possibly worked during the Roman period. But it was during the industrialisation of the rest of the country that the industry peaked, and hardly any worthwhile deposit was left untapped. In consequence, there are few places where you cannot find evidence of this exploitation, but strangely this only adds another

Semer Water in winter, Addlebrough
in the background (Walk 33)

dimension to the appeal of exploring the area.

Until it was dismantled in 1964, Wensleydale too had its railway, which ran all the way to Garsdale Head, where it connected with the Settle–Carlisle line. Although it remained in existence for less than a century, the railway was a boon to both farming and a small textile industry by providing a ready conduit for export, as well as opening the valley to the early tourism of the Victorians.

But even before that, Wensleydale had a major thoroughfare in the form of the Richmond–Lancaster turnpike, and for this reason of all the dales it is the only one to have a market town of any size in its higher reaches. In appearance too Wensleydale is different to the other dales, being broad and flat-bottomed for much of its length, where its pastures supported a much richer farming industry than was possible in the other dales. There was mining for both lead and coal as well as quarrying for stone, but these were scattered in small pockets, bringing diversity of occupation rather than the focus of an all-consuming enterprise.

Nidderdale is the one major valley that no longer has a through road, although in earlier days strings of mules and pack-horses crossed the bleak moorland pass into Coverdale. Nidderdale's exclusion from the Yorkshire Dales National Park appears to have been because of the chain of reservoirs built to supply the

33

expanding population of Bradford, but although something was undoubtedly lost in the flooding, few would strenuously argue that the lakes do not now bring another element of loveliness to its upper corners. With limestone gorges at its heart, stretches of luxuriant woodland beside the river, and overlooked by the striking formations of Brimham Rocks, it displays some of the greatest diversity in the whole of the Dales.

The Howgills, quite literally, stand apart from all else, a great mass of green hill rising abruptly from the deep valleys that separate them from the neighbouring high ground. The uncompromisingly steep buttressing flanks are undoubtedly a deterrent to their greater popularity, but the effort of getting to the tops is rewarded by superb panoramas and long, undulating walks on broad grassy ridges.

THE YORKSHIRE DALES NATIONAL PARK

Centred on the core of this unique area is the Yorkshire Dales National Park, created in 1954 and the seventh of the UK's national parks. The then omission of Nidderdale, Mallerstang, the Howgills and the western outlying hills was heavily criticised, for although beyond the bounds of Yorkshire, they are geologically and geographically connected and equally deserving of protection. Forty years were to pass before Nidderdale was finally designated an Area of Outstanding Natural Beauty (AONB), but it was not until August 2016 that the national park's boundaries were extended to encompass the remaining areas.

The additional areas increased the park's size by almost a quarter to 2178km² (841 square miles) to make it the country's third largest, with the Nidderdale AONB adding a further 600km² (233 square miles). Somewhat less than half of this is actively managed as agricultural land, while the rest consists largely of open country and moorland. Historic land use, geography and climate mitigate against extensive areas of woodland, and little more than 3% is covered by trees, the largest single area being the coniferous plantations encircling the higher reaches of Langstrothdale.

Because of the geology, extensive bodies of water are also notable by their absence, and in fact only two natural lakes of significance occur in the whole of the Dales – Malham Tarn and Semer Water. However, the gritstone valleys in the south and east harbour a number of man-made reservoirs, built to sustain the industrial towns of West Yorkshire.

The park's resident population is around 20,000 – less than 30 people per square mile. But this figure is swelled by an estimated 3.3 million a day, and half a million overnight visitors each year, increasing the resident population by, on average, almost a half. And while most people live in one of the three small towns lying wholly

Distinctive signs mark the boundary of the national park (Walk 8)

The national park takes the Swaledale as its emblem (Walk 30)

within its boundaries – Sedbergh, Hawes and Grassington – few of even the remotest dales are totally devoid of habitation. Picturesque villages and hamlets are scattered along the major valleys, with small steadings to be found everywhere, right up into the highest reaches. This all might seem like rather a lot of people, but wander away from the main centres, even on a bank holiday weekend, and you can spend a day on the tops with hardly a soul about.

Almost all of today's roads follow ancient lines of travel, as do many of the paths and tracks that lie away from the tarmac. There are few main roads, however, and the majority of the narrow lanes are relatively traffic free and a delight to walk, cycle or ride. In addition, there are in excess of 3200km (2000 miles) of designated footpaths, bridleways and tracks, which contour the dales, climb the intervening hills and criss-cross the open moors. And, following the implementation of the CROW Act in 2000, around 1087km² (about 420 square miles), including the majority of the upland area, is now designated open access land.

Much of the countryside encompassed within the legislation is upland moor and heath, and is identified on OS Explorer maps by peach-coloured (open land) and light-green (woodland) tints. Access points on the ground are usually identified by a circular brown-and-white symbol of a walking figure. Within these areas

you have a right to wander (but not cycle), even where there is no path, but there are responsibilities too. These are generally common sense, such as following the Countryside Code (see www.openaccess.gov. uk) and being careful not to cause damage. Dogs are sometimes permitted too, but should be on a close lead near livestock and during the bird-breeding season (1 March to 31 July). However, on many of the grouse moors dogs are not allowed at any time other than on designated public footpaths. Landowners are entitled to suspend or restrict access for short periods, for example during the grouse-shooting season or while heather and gorse burning takes place. There may also be restrictions for conservation purposes. Such closures are notified in advance and should be respected, but do not affect any public rights of way that may run across the land.

PRACTICALITIES

Although none of the routes described in this book is technically demanding, many venture onto upland moors where paths may be vague or non-existent, and conditions can be very different from those in the valleys. The weather can rapidly deteriorate at any time of year, and inexperienced walkers should be aware that it is easy to become disorientated in mist. However, taking a few simple and common-sense precautions will help ensure you get the best out of the day.

Navigation and maps

The mapping extracts (1:50,000) accompanying each walk in this guidebook are provided to indicate the general outline of the route and are not intended as a substitute for the map itself. The context of the wider

Take heed of any warning signs (Walk 9)

area will not only add to the enjoyment of identifying neighbouring hills and other features, but is vital should you wander off course or need to find a quick way back.

On the open moors and hills, paths may be indistinct or non-existent and, particularly in poor visibility, the terrain may pose navigational problems for inexperienced walkers. You should therefore be competent in the use of map and compass and, while a GPS receiver can be a useful additional aid, you should know how to use it and be aware of its shortcomings. Remember, too, to carry spare batteries. Be aware of your limitations, and do not start out if anticipated conditions are likely to be beyond your experience, and should the weather deteriorate unexpectedly, always be prepared turn back.

The area is covered by Ordnance Survey maps at both 1:25,000 and 1:50,000 scales, the larger scale showing a greater detail that is often invaluable. The key maps for the walks in this guide are: Explorer OL2 – Yorkshire Dales (Southern & Western areas); Explorer OL30 – Yorkshire Dales

(Northern & Central areas); Explorer OL19 – Howgill Fells & Upper Eden Valley; and Explorer 298 – Nidderdale.

Careful planning

Plan your walk in advance, bearing in mind your party's capabilities and the anticipated weather conditions for the day. The times given in this guidebook for each walk are based on Naismith's Rule, and are provided merely as a guide. They make no allowance for stops along the way, and in practice your time may be significantly greater, since it will depend on your level of fitness, ability to cope with the particular terrain, and other factors such as weather.

The amount of height gain, poor conditions underfoot and lousy weather can add considerably to both the time and effort needed to complete a walk, and it is a good idea to make your own estimate, adapting Naismith's Rule to match your own performance. Naismith's Rule basically takes into account distance and height gain, allowing one hour for every 5km (3 miles) and a further half hour for each 300m ascended. By monitoring your own performance over a period to determine appropriate personal times for each element of the calculation, you can achieve a reasonably reliable formula that suits your own level of capability. Having said that, particularly if you are out alone, it is also a good idea to leave a note of your intended route and return time with someone (*not* sitting on the

dashboard of your car as an open invitation to a thief).

Clothing and footwear

Wear appropriate clothing and footwear and carry a comfortable rucksack. The variability of British weather can pack all four seasons into a single day – sun, rain, wind and snow – with the temperature bobbing up and down like a yo-yo. All this makes deciding what to wear for a day on the hills potentially more difficult than choosing an outfit for a wedding. The comprehensive advice is to be prepared for everything, and with today's technical fabrics, this is not as daft as it may seem.

Lightweight jackets and trousers can be both effectively wind- and waterproof without being too cumbersome should the weather improve. Efficient underlayers wick away the damp to keep you warm and dry, and throwing in a fleece takes up little extra room. Good-quality socks will help keep feet comfortable and warm, and don't forget gloves and a hat. In summer, a sun hat and sunscreen lotion offer necessary protection against UV, but shorts aren't always a good idea, particularly where there are nettles and brambles.

Whether you choose leather or fabric boots is a matter of personal preference, but you should ensure that they are waterproof rather than merely water resistant. They should, of course, be comfortable, as well as offering good ankle support and grip underfoot. Finally, note that mobile phone coverage is at best patchy.

Food and drink

A number of these walks take you past a pub or a café at some stage, but if you intend to rely on them for a snack or meal, do check in advance that they will be open. It is, in any case, always advisable to pack emergency rations, in case your walk takes longer than anticipated. Also carry plenty to drink, particularly when the weather is warmer, as dehydration can be a significant problem. Drinking from streams is not always a good idea, and in limestone country they can be something of a rarity in any case.

Taking your car

If you travel to the start of the walk by car, remember that the roads, never intended for today's traffic volumes, are generally narrow, have many bends and several very steep hills. Extra care is also needed because slow-moving farm vehicles, animals, pedestrians, horse riders and cyclists may lie around any corner. And, while you might be enjoying a leisurely drive soaking up the beauty of the countryside, the car behind could contain a local just going about his daily business, so be a courteous driver and pull over as soon as it is convenient to allow faster-moving traffic to safely pass.

Wherever possible, use official car parks. This helps to reduce congestion, avoid obstruction and protect verges, and gives a measure of protection against car crime. The revenue from national park car parks is used to improve services for visitors to the park. If there is no car park available, please park considerately, and ensure that you do not obstruct field or farm access or cause damage.

Leaving your car behind

However, leaving the car behind not only helps the environment, but opens a wealth of other opportunities for your visit. Instead of confining yourself to circular walks, which most of us accept as the norm for a day out, you can broaden your horizons in walking from one dale to the next. Combined with an overnight stay or two you can truly become a traveller, and begin to appreciate the relationships between the different valleys. The Dales offers several real alternatives to using the car. There is a frequent rail service along the Settle–Carlisle line serving the upper Ribble Valley, Dent Head and Garsdale. Regular bus services run into most of the popular dales, with additional services at weekends and during the summer. Full details are available from the Dales Bus website (www.dalesbus.org).

Cycling is another environmentally friendly way of getting about. Take your own bike, perhaps leaving the car at one of the fringe car parks, or hire one when you get there. You will find useful information on the Cycle the Yorkshire Dales website (www.cyclethedales.org.uk).

Narrow lanes and a tractor leave little room for walkers (Walk 16)

A Norman stronghold, Castlehaw was built around 1070 to control passage along the valley of the Rawthey (Walk 1)

If you have the time, spend a couple of relaxing days in the area rather than stressfully travelling back and forth on day visits. There is a wealth of inviting bed and breakfast, hotel and inn accommodation, as well as campsites, and the area has a wonderful reputation for its food. Check out www.yorkshiredales.org/accommodation.

USING THIS GUIDE

The walks in this guidebook are for everyone, from novices to experienced ramblers, although newcomers to walking are advised to develop their abilities and confidence on the shorter walks before progressing onto the more demanding routes. However, none of the walks in this book is technically difficult, and in good weather they pose few navigational problems.

Simple skills such as the ability to use a map and compass will help keep you on the right track, and map and compass are essential in poor visibility.

The network of public footpaths and tracks is extensive, and signposts and waymarks are generally well positioned to confirm the route. On the upper moors, and indeed across many of the valley meadows, the actual line of the path is not always distinct, but the way is often discernible along a 'trod'. Defined as a 'mark made by treading', a trod, by its nature, becomes more obvious the more it is walked, and indeed may develop over time as a path. But on the upper slopes it is a less tangible thing, a slight flattening of the grass or reeds punctuated with an occasional boot print. It may differ from a sheep track only in that it has purposeful direction and requires an element of concentration to stay on the right course.

The walks described in detail in this volume range in distance from 3½ to 11½ miles (5.6 to 18.5km), and there are suggestions for devising longer days by combining routes. While the lengthier walks require an appropriate degree of physical fitness, none demand more than an ability to walk. The Dales are hilly rather than mountainous, and with gains in altitude during the walks of between 80m (262ft) and 855m (2805ft), climbs are generally moderate, with any steep sections usually brief. And in any case, the captivating scenery so begs attention that frequent pauses for retrospective admiration are almost mandatory.

Almost all of the walks are circular, many beginning from recognised car parks with a public toilet nearby. However, public transport in the Dales, particularly during the summer months and at weekends, now offers a real alternative for reaching many of the more popular locations, and increases the opportunity for adapting and devising many satisfying 'one way' walks around the routes described here.

Yorkshire's warm hospitality is renowned, and you'll find welcoming pubs, cafés and tea shops throughout the area, although it is always a good idea to check opening times in advance if you are relying on somewhere for a meal.

Details of the terrain and nature of the walk, together with the local facilities available, are given in the information box at the start of each walk.

PART 1
THE HOWGILL FELLS

Dropping over 200m, Cautley Spout is England's highest waterfall (Walk 6)

WALK 1

Sedbergh and the River Rawthey

Start	Sedbergh (SD657921)
Distance	5 miles (8km)
Height gain	145m (476ft)
Time	2hr
Terrain	Field paths and trods
OS map	Explorer OL19 – Howgill Fells & Upper Eden Valley
Refreshments	Pubs and cafés in Sedbergh
Toilets	Beside car parks
Parking	Car parks in Sedbergh (pay and display)

Above Sedbergh, the narrowing valley of the River Rawthey becomes squeezed between the soaring hills of the Howgills and the lower slopes of Rise Hill and Baugh Fell. This undemanding ramble begins across the lower slopes past the castle that oversaw the town's early development, and returns beside the river by the ruin of a more recent lookout from the 19th century. For a longer day, the route can be linked with Walk 2 to include an exploration of the lower part of the valley.

From the junction by St Andrew's Church, walk east along Main Street through the centre of town. Meeting Long Lane at the end, go left and immediately left again, beside Westwood Books, up a track signed to Castlehaw. Breaking from the trees above the town, the mound of **Castlehaw** comes into view across to the right. The access is over a stile as the track shortly curves right.

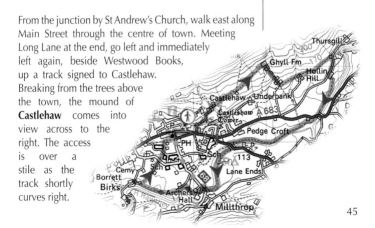

45

CASTLEHAW

An early Norman stronghold dating from the end of the 11th century, the castle held a commanding position above the entrance to the Rawthey valley. Exploiting a small outcrop, the steep-sided motte, on which stood a defensible wooden tower, still dominates the site, and would have been further defended by a deep ditch and wooden palisade. The living area lay within the bailey, the lower apron projecting to the west, and contained the lord's hall as well as quarters for his retainers and dependants. With the consolidation of Norman rule it became redundant, and was never rebuilt in stone as were those further to the north. It was, however, brought back into use during the last war as a lookout for the Royal Observer Corps.

Return to the track and continue to Castlehaw Farm, swinging left in front of the barns and then right across a stream past Howgills Bunk Barn. Through a gate, walk ahead across the fields beyond, contouring above the bottom fence to an isolated barn. Keep going, later crossing a couple of ladder stiles to find the boundary now on your left.

Bounded by the abruptly rising slopes of the Howgills, the views are captivating. Ahead, the great rounded hump of Baugh Fell falls to the foot of Garsdale, while to the right, Frostrow Fells prelude the higher ground of Aye Gill Pike.

Overlooking Sedbergh, Winder is the southernmost top of the Howgill Fells

Reaching **Ghyll Farm**, exit through a stable yard and follow its track away to the right. At a fork, just beyond a cattle-grid, bear left into Stone Hill Farm, looking for a small gate in the right corner into a cobbled yard fronting the house. Leave through a field gate at the bottom and walk left at the field edge past the barns. Over a footbridge, continue to the next farm, **Hollin Hill**.

Bear left past the farmhouse and through the yard. In the field beyond, bear right across the hillside to a stile. Over a second stile, keep going, later passing the top end of a truncated wall to find a stile just above a white house. Walk down to emerge beside it onto Buckbank Lane.

Turn right to **Buckbank Farm** and enter the yard. Go right between the barns and then left beside the silage store to the field. Follow the perimeter down and continue above the wooded ravine of the River Rawthey to meet the main road at **Straight Bridge**.

The way continues beside the river through a gap stile opposite to the A684 at **New Bridge**. Over the Rawthey, turn through a kissing-gate and carry on downstream, emerging by another bridge at **Millthrop**. Cross back to find a gate, just beyond the drive to Millthrop Mill.

Strike out past the mill to enter a small wood above the river. Watch for the waymarked path swinging right between sunken walls, at the end of which, walk forward and take the right-most of the forking paths to a gate at the edge of the trees. Go left and carry on beyond the corner of the wood and the ruin of an octagonal tower.

Known as the **Pepper Pot** and dating from the end of the 19th century, the tower was a gazebo or summerhouse within the gardens of Akay House. The house was demolished just before the Second World War, but the tower, originally rising to two storeys, was left to crumble in its own good time. The folly became the scene of excitement when a cow wandered in, managing to reach the first floor, and an old photograph shows it gazing bemusedly from the window.

The path falls from the field to rejoin the river, running past one of Sedbergh School's rugby pitches to a kissing-gate. To carry on with Walk 2, keep ahead up to the path around Birks House to come out on **Birks Lane**.

Otherwise, swing away from the river, heading upfield towards a barn. Emerging onto a track, follow it out to Busk Lane. Through a kissing-gate opposite, climb to another gate at the top of a rise and, crossing a path, continue beside a sports field. Swing right past the cricket pavilion to come out onto Finkle Street beside **St Andrew's churchyard**.

ST ANDREW'S CHURCH, SEDBERGH

Low and wide, St Andrew's is typical of many Dales churches and seems completely at one with the surrounding countryside. Its most notable feature is the stained glass filling the eastern window, installed at the end of the 19th century by one of the town's great benefactors, Mrs Upton-Cottrell-Dormer of Ingmire Hall. In 1906, she presented the town with Queen's Gardens to commemorate Victoria's long reign, but the window here was given in memory of her husband and parents. Depicting Jesus calling his first disciples, Simon Peter and Andrew, to be 'fishers of men', it was designed by Victor Milner, considered to be one of the finest craftsmen of his day, and made by Watsons of Baker Street in London.

WALK 2

The Rivers Rawthey and
Lune from Sedbergh

Start	Sedbergh (SD657921)
Distance	6½ miles (10.5km)
Height gain	215m (705ft)
Time	2hr30
Terrain	Field paths and trods; a stream crossing may involve a paddle, return along a lane
OS map	Explorer OL19 – Howgill Fells & Upper Eden Valley
Refreshments	Pubs and cafés in Sedbergh
Toilets	Beside car parks
Parking	Car parks in Sedbergh (pay and display)

Nestling under the Howgill Fells, Sedbergh is a popular starting point for high-level walks onto the hills, but is equally well placed for many gentler rambles amongst the lower slopes. Downstream, the Dee and Rawthey combine to meet the River Lune, a corner criss-crossed by paths and quiet lanes that link the old mills and scattered valley farms that helped foster trade at the ancient market town. Amongst the sights are two impressive examples of Victorian engineering – viaducts that carried the former Ingleton railway above the rivers. The walk can be undertaken on its own, or treated as an extension to the previous ramble.

Beginning from the junction on Main Street by St Andrew's Church, head down Finkle Street. Just beyond the roundabout at Back Lane, turn along a path between the graveyard and Sedbergh School's cricket field.

Go left at the corner past the pavilion and continue over a crossing path, dropping through a kissing-gate across grass to emerge onto Busk Lane. Opposite, a sign to Birks directs you along a track beside the rugby pitches. Reaching a barn, bear off right through a wooden kissing-gate and carry on along a field, where a

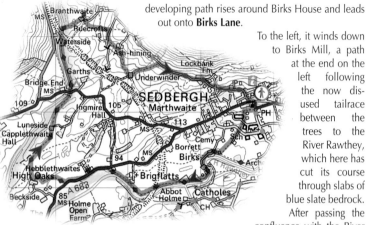

developing path rises around Birks House and leads out onto **Birks Lane**.

To the left, it winds down to Birks Mill, a path at the end on the left following the now disused tailrace between the trees to the River Rawthey, which here has cut its course through slabs of blue slate bedrock. After passing the confluence with the River Dee flowing from Dentdale, the way breaks out at the edge of fields, where there is a fine view to Winder, the southwestern outpost of the Howgill Fells. Having clambered over the embankment of a disused railway line, the path becomes enclosed behind Brigflatts and eventually leads out to the main road.

> The **railway**, carried high above the river on a striking cast-iron skew bridge, ran from Ingleton to Lowgill at the foot of the Lune Gorge, where it connected with the main west coast route to Carlisle.

Cross and follow the road left past the entrance to Ingmire Caravan Park, continuing for a further ¼ mile (400m) to find a path leaving through a kissing-gate and signed to High Oaks. Negotiating a stream at the far side of the field, bear left over the shoulder of a small hillock.

At the far corner, a hedged path leads to the cottages at **High Oaks**. Go right and then left to the corner of a track. Turn right between the buildings to a second junction and there walk right again, climbing away on a hedged grass track.

Through a small gate at the end, a sign directs you right to Lincoln's Inn Bridge. Ignore a path shortly signed off to Ingmire, and instead, continue to a gate in the far corner. Carry on at the field edge and then along a hedged track to Luneside.

Wind right through the farmyard, as if to leave along the access track, but almost immediately bear off through a gate on the left. Head for a lone ash and then follow the fence to a stile, the path falling beyond to accompany the riverbank up to **Lincoln's Inn Bridge**.

Lincoln's Inn Bridge was built in the 17th century

51

Go along the road a short distance to the right, crossing to a track signed through a gate to Low Branthwaite. Before long the imposing **Lune Viaduct** at Waterside comes into view, but before it is Crosdale Beck, which, after rain, may involve a paddle.

THE LUNE VIADUCT

Part of the same Ingleton branch line encountered earlier, the Lune Viaduct has three towering stone arches either side of a massive, cast-iron central span. The engineer was Joseph Locke, who started out as an apprentice under George Stephenson on the Stockton & Darlington and Liverpool & Manchester railways. Early railways avoided hills and followed the snaking canals, but Locke gained a reputation for his bold use of gradients to achieve shorter routes. This dramatically reduced both construction cost and time, and was matched by increasingly powerful locomotives. The Ingleton project was one of the last upon which he worked, for Locke died suddenly at the age of 55 from appendicitis, in 1860, just a year before the line opened.

After passing beneath the bridge, bear right up the bank, signs at the top directing you right to a gate and stile. Carry on above Crosdale Beck to emerge onto a track from **Low Branthwaite Farm**. Go right, leaving immediately beyond a bridge over a stile on the right.

Climb left to a small, gated stile, from which the onward path is signed to the Height of Winder – indeed, Winder itself looms straight ahead as you walk up the field. Walk on, cutting the bottom right corner and climbing to a small gate. Bear left upfield, passing buildings and over a crossing track to a gated stile in the top wall onto **Slacks Lane**.

Walk right for 150m to a gate on the left beneath a sign to Underwinder. Head out alongside a couple of fields to cottages at **Ash-hining**. Turn into the yard, but exit immediately through a second gate on the right. Bear right across to a ladder stile beside a gate in the far wall, and contour the hillside to reach yet another farm and cottages at **Underwinder**.

Entering the yard, go right, and then turn left through a gate beside the end cottage, walking up past its garden

Sunset on the Howgills

to the field behind. Climb away at the perimeter of a couple of fields to emerge through a gate at the top onto **Howgill Lane**. To the right, it eventually takes you back into Sedbergh.

WALK 3
Winder, Calders and the Calf

Start	Sedbergh (SD657921)
Distance	9¾ miles (15.7km)
Height gain	855m (2805ft)
Time	4hr45
Terrain	Indistinct upland trods; a stream crossing may involve a paddle, return along a lane.
OS map	Explorer OL19 – Howgill Fells & Upper Eden Valley
Refreshments	Pubs and cafés in Sedbergh
Toilets	Beside car parks
Parking	Car parks in Sedbergh (pay and display)

The grassy flanks of the Howgills rear as a formidable backdrop to Sedbergh, the peripheral summits serving as stepping-stones to the cluster of higher summits behind. The first pull is the most exacting, and leads over Winder and Calders onto the Calf, the highest point of the group of hills. This climb has been a traditional challenge for pupils of famous Sedbergh School, and is immortalised in the refrain of their ancient song:

…'Tis the hills that are stood around us, unchanged since our days began. It is Cautley, Calf and WINDER, that make the Sedbergh man.

This walk follows the path trodden by countless Sedbergh School lads, and now girls, onto the tops, dropping back over White Fell to return along the more gentle flanks of the Lune valley.

Begin from the junction of Main Street and Finkle Street, by St Andrew's Church at the western end of the town, and head past the post office in the direction of Kendal.

Take the first street on the right, just past the Dalesman pub. Follow it up behind the town, winding above playing fields and past the houses beyond. As they fizzle out, bear off right on a track signed as a permissive path up

to **Lockbank Farm**.

At the top, walk through a gate to the right of the building facing you, from which a short track rises to the open fell. Go left beside the wall, but almost immediately bear off right on a path that determinedly attacks the southern flank of **Winder**.

Fragmenting higher up, it offers a choice of routes to the summit, but none escapes the steep climb. The compensation, however, is the splendid view opening behind, of Middleton Fell, Great Coum, Whernside and

Rise Hill, while over to the southeast is the great mass of Baugh Fell.

Eventually, the lessening gradient heralds the approaching top, and the concrete trig column suddenly springs into view. Beside it is a topograph, erected to commemorate the millennium, and which helps identify the surrounding hills visible from this superb vantage.

The onward path runs ahead in gradual descent along the northeast rib of the hill, falling to meet a lower path from Lockbank Farm that has bypassed the summit. Beyond a shallow saddle, take the left fork and climb on towards **Arant Haw**.

After another stiff pull, the ground abruptly levels, but, despite the significantly greater altitude, there is no trig column, just a melancholy pile of pebbles, which has more the appearance of an abandoned campfire hearth than a cairn.

Bear right along a broad grassy shoulder, the great sweeping ridges that buttress the western flanks of the Howgills presenting a dramatic sight. Unhurriedly descending, rejoin the path that contoured the southeastern slope and continue over Rowantree Grains, where yawning gullies bite deep into the hill from both sides.

Beyond, the pace settles once more into a steady plod up the steepening southern ridge of **Calders**. The top is marked by a pile of stones, notable only because of the lack of any obvious source of building material. With all the strenuous work now behind you, turn left and enjoy the undulating ½ mile (800m) stroll over the intermediate Bram Rigg Top onto **the Calf**.

There is remarkable consistency in the heights of the main **Howgill summits**, and the Calf only manages a bare 2m supremacy over Calders. It is, however, graced with a trig column and, just to the side in a shallow scrape, is a small tarn. The views are truly magnificent, and reach out west to the distant jagged peaks of Lakeland and around Morecambe Bay to the shimmering Celtic sea.

Turning around to the east brings in Baugh Fell and Wild Boar Fell, while behind, the long spine of watershed hills stretches north past High Seat to far-off Nine Standards Rigg.

Continue past the trig, but then bear left off the main path, making for the lower, flat-topped outrider of **White Fell Head**. Over to the right, the eye is drawn into the head of Langdale, which slices north through the hills for almost six miles (9.7km) to meet the infant River Lune.

At a later fork, keep left, curving around the southern edge of the plateau to begin a descent along the drawn-out tongue of White Fell. As the gradient steepens, there is an impressive view across the deep fold of Calf Beck, the ground falling to the confluence of streams in the intimacy of the valley below.

A developing track drops to a stony ford across **Long Rigg Beck**, which after rain may frustrate a dry-shod crossing, and those carrying a small towel might then be glad of their foresight.

Looking across Brant Fell to Arant Haw

As the way rounds the apron of Castley Knotts, pause to glance back at the superb setting of the upper valley, for all too suddenly the track turns a corner and leaves the upper fell to run between the confining walls of the lower enclosures.

Reaching a junction above **Castley Farm** you have a choice. Either bear right and follow the track out to Four Lane Ends, or cut across the fields to Gate Side, both routes taking you out to **Howgill Lane**.

If opting for the fields, turn down towards the farm and then swing right past the end of the farmhouse, leaving the lower yard through the right-most of two gates into the field behind. Walk away beside the right-hand fence, going right in the next field to another gate. Bear right to a ladder stile and then keep ahead, dipping to cross a stream. A grass track leads to the lower of two gates, through which skirt below farm buildings to a final ladder stile.

Emerging onto Howgill Lane, go left, following it down to a bridge across **Chapel Beck**, the stream you forded earlier. Through a gate over to the right is the tiny church of Holy Trinity, set within a pretty graveyard shaded by neatly trimmed yews. The way back to Sedbergh, however, lies with the main lane, branching left at a fork a mile (1.6km) further on, and eventually picking up your outward route at Lockbank.

WALK 4

*Carlin Gill and Fell Head from
Fairmile Gate*

Start	Fairmile Gate (SD629977)
Distance	6¼ miles (10.1km)
Height gain	570m (1870ft)
Time	3hr
Terrain	Begin along a lane, a short scramble through a narrow gorge followed by indistinct upland trods; Carlin Gill can be impassable after heavy rain.
OS map	Explorer OL19 – Howgill Fells & Upper Eden Valley
Refreshments	None
Toilets	None
Parking	Limited roadside parking north of Fairmile Gate

Sedbergh and Cautley are the most popular centres for walks onto the Howgill Fells, largely because of their ease of access and proximity to the highest points. However, this route exploiting the winding corridor of Carlin Gill is one of the most dramatic, and reveals something of the subtle variances of character concealed within the steep folds of these hunched-up hills. It begins along a serpentine, drawn-out valley that delves into the massif, creating an air of remoteness almost from the very start. The way soon becomes increasingly rugged, a sharp contrast to the grassy slopes above, while the head of the valley is abruptly closed by a waterfall that demands a scrambling climb to overcome. To the fit and agile, it will present little difficulty, but even if you do no more than admire the spectacle and retrace your steps down the valley, you will undoubtedly enjoy the day.

It is not possible to sensibly park a car beside the lane south of Fairmile Gate, but beyond there are several opportunities to pull off onto the verge.

It doesn't matter where you stop along here, for the walk continues north along the lane as far as Carlingill Bridge. On the ground it gently meanders, but the map

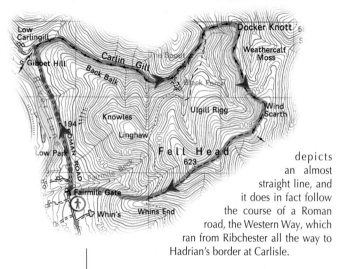

depicts an almost straight line, and it does in fact follow the course of a Roman road, the Western Way, which ran from Ribchester all the way to Hadrian's border at Carlisle.

At Low Borrowbridge, less than a couple of miles (3.2km) beyond Carlingill Bridge, is the site of a **Roman fort**, although hardly any trace is visible today. There are, however, some contemporary stones to be found in the riverbank, which are the remains of a bridge abutment that spanned the Lune.

Ahead stretches the Lune gorge, a delightful cleft dividing the hills either side, the river snaking in a glassy ribbon at its base. To the left is Grayrigg Common, while to the right the land rises steeply to Linghaw and Knowles, outlying tongues of Fell Head, the objective of the walk. Eventually the lane drops beneath ominously named Gibbet Hill to the bridge at **Low Carlingill**.

Turn off immediately before the bridge, following a path up beside the stream. The waterside route occasionally switches banks, although a higher path pegs the southern slopes to the foot of Small Gill. The steep hillsides alternately step back to reveal a broader valley floor where the main stream meanders across pebble beds, but then the flanks close in, ushering you to the heart of the mountains.

Looking back along Carlin Gill from below the Spout

Beyond the confluence of Small Gill the path is squeezed out of the ravine's base, picking its way across the steep, flanking scree on the left. ▶

Carry on past Black Force, a boisterous stream fully deserving of its name, which cascades from a steep, dark gully that reaches back to the yet unseen flanks of Fell Head. Beyond the wooded narrowing, the path drops back to the stream, periodically swapping sides and clambering over rocks to pick the best way through to the base of **the Spout**, a 10m fall blocking the head of the gorge.

There is a choice of escape routes out of the ravine, the most direct being an abrupt scramble up a rib of rock to the left of the fall, and which leads to easier ground beside the stream in the upper valley. The alternative is to tackle the very steep grassy slope on the right, to reach a higher path coming from the head of Black Force, and which drops to ford Great Ulgill Beck. While it might initially seem a better option to those unskilled in scrambling, it too demands sure-footedness, and is not recommended in wet weather when the ground can be dangerously slippery.

Surprisingly, the cleft below is well wooded, the precipitous sides giving protection from both the elements and the incessant nibbling of sheep.

Whichever way out you choose, continue into the upper valley, which impressively opens as a great amphitheatre, a stark contrast to the narrow confines below. Meeting the watershed, beyond which Uldale falls away, look for the **Blakethwaite Stone**, a small boulder incised with a bench mark and initials indicating the old boundary between Yorkshire and Westmorland. Swing right to pick up a grass trod climbing to a shallow col between the grassy hills of Hand Lake and Docker Knott.

Gaining the crest, camber right again and follow the broad ridge up to the gently rounded dome of **Docker Knott**, inconspicuously marked by a couple of stones. A grand viewpoint, it overlooks the valley of Churn Gill, which runs almost due north parallel to Uldale. To the west is Carlin Gill, while ahead to the south, the rest of the day's walk is laid open to view.

Bearing right, a trod takes you along the ridge, dropping to another saddle before rising to Over Sale. Carry on across the springy turf up the slope of Wind Scarth and, as the gradient then eases, curve gently right onto **Fell Head**, its top marked by a half-respectable cairn, no mean achievement in a landscape largely devoid of stones.

White Fell Head and Calders from Fell Head

Fell Head is a sublime spot from which to ponder the Howgill Fells' topography – broad, interconnecting saddles that link each of the central summits. To the southeast, almost 1½ miles (2.4km) away, is the highest point of the complex, the Calf, while dotted around are the lesser heights, all formidably defended by steep grassy slopes. Further afield, the eye is drawn down Long Rigg Beck and past Killington Lake into the lower Lune valley, and slightly to the right is the Kent Estuary, crossed by the distant railway viaduct at the head of Morecambe Bay. Further round are the Lakeland mountains, while to the east can be seen Wild Boar Fell and the northern Pennines.

With nothing left to do but go down, carry on past the summit, falling to a lower hill marked by a respectfully smaller cairn. There bear left, heading west of south in the direction of the distant Lune viaduct, picking up a trod that drops determinedly towards **Whins End**.

The view remains captivating, drawing the eye into the valley on the left, which falls from the steep, scarred slopes of Bush Howe. High up, a patch of dark scree has the vague form of a horse, but this is no man-made feature, merely a random creation of nature.

Eventually the gradient eases and crosses a contouring path, but carry on along the descending tongue. Avoid being drawn into the valley on the left, and bear right, aiming for the corner of the intake wall above Fairmile Beck. Follow the bracken-clad gully down to meet the lane beside the bridge at Fairmile Gate.

WALK 5

*The River Rawthey from the
Cross Keys Inn*

Start	The Cross Keys Inn beside the A683, 4½ miles (7.2km) northeast of Sedbergh (SD698969)
Distance	5 miles (8km)
Height gain	170m (558ft)
Time	2hr
Terrain	Field trods and tracks
OS map	Explorer OL19 – Howgill Fells & Upper Eden Valley
Refreshments	The Cross Keys Inn
Toilets	None
Parking	Limited roadside parking near the Cross Keys Inn

The walk there and back into the base of the valley to view Cautley Spout can be an objective in itself, but if you're looking for something a little longer without venturing onto higher ground, your explorations can be extended with this walk downstream along the Rawthey, returning, without too much climbing, along the contours of the hillside, from which there is a splendid view into the higher reaches of the dale.

From the small lay-by beside the lane at the Cross Keys Inn, drop to a footbridge over the River Rawthey and head downstream on its opposite bank. The path later curves into the valley, below **Cautley Crag**, towards the falls, where for the energetic a path climbs steeply to them.

After exploring the cascades, return to the footbridge at the foot of Cautley Holme Beck, passed on the way up. On the opposite bank, turn down towards the confluence, but then swing away between walls to pass through a gate. Just beyond, leave the main bridleway, branching left to a second gate. Continue past a barn across the fields towards the farm at **Cautley Thwaite**. Walk by the end of the farm-house and leave along a walled track, prettily lined with daffodils in early spring.

Across the valley, running above the modern road around the flank of Bluecaster, is the **old coach road** connecting Sedbergh and Kirkby Stephen. The house seen on the hillside was once an inn to serve passing trade. Old stories tell of coachmen having too many nips to keep out the cold, and then dozing off at the reins, leaving the horses to find their own way. On one occasion, many tears were shed when a barrel of beer slipped off the delivery wagon, rolling free down the hillside to smash on the rocks below.

Continue along the track, curving with it in front of a barn to cross a bridge spanning the river by **Wardses**. Immediately over the bridge, go through a narrow gate on the right and head downstream across the fields to the next farm at **In Close**. Passing a barn, bear left to a gate and follow a path up to a low waypost. Veer right to join a tarmac drive and keep left where it shortly splits. Approaching a house, leave through a gated gap on the left and cross the field to a track by a barn. Go right and then bear left across a smaller paddock to reach a bridge across the river.

Back on the northern bank, bear left to find a path slanting up the wooded slope above the river, in a while, breaking out into the fields above. Continue across the hillside, picking up a grass path that eventually passes a ruined steading, **Brow Side**. Walk just beyond to meet a path dropping from the right.

Turn up the path to a stile, over which go right and follow a gently undulating path at the foot of the open

Cautley Holme Beck meets the River Rawthey

Bounded on the one hand by Baugh and Wild Boar fells and on the other by Wandale Hill and Harter Fell, a marvellous view extends right up the valley to the watershed.

hillside, later passing through occasional gates in the rugged walls that divide the rough upper pastures. ◀

Eventually the path reaches a gate back out of the intake. Carry on at the edge of the open fell, ultimately falling to meet your outward path above the barn at **Cautley Beck**. Retrace your steps to the bridge and follow the path back to the Cross Keys Inn.

WALK 6
Cautley Crag and the Calf

Start	The Cross Keys Inn beside the A683, 4½ miles (7.2km) northeast of Sedbergh (SD698969)
Distance	7 miles (11.3km)
Height gain	640m (2100ft)
Time	3hr15
Terrain	Indistinct upland trods with steep, rugged section demanding care on descent
OS map	Explorer OL19 – Howgill Fells & Upper Eden Valley
Refreshments	The Cross Keys Inn
Toilets	None
Parking	Limited roadside parking near the Cross Keys Inn

Approached from almost any direction, the Howgills present a formidably steep face to those challenging their airy heights. But these hills are meant to be savoured, and their arduous slopes force a slow pace that encourages contemplation of the subtly changing panoramas revealed with increasing height. Once on the tops, however, their interconnecting saddles and unbounded ridges provide relatively easy passage between summits, and offer endless opportunities for exploration. This is just such a walk, the hard work of the initial stages more than amply rewarded with captivating views from just about every point along the way.

From the roadside parking near the Cross Keys Inn, drop to a bridge across the Rawthey and head downstream below the steep snout of Ben End. Approaching Cautley Holme Beck, the path curves into the sweeping valley below **Cautley Crag**, a vast amphitheatre scooped out of the hillside.

The way begins to rise over great grassy humps of moraine debris left by retreating glaciers, steadily steepening as it works its way into the valley, where the creaming cascades of Cautley Spout can be seen high up at the far end of the crumbling crags.

Many places within the Howgills are awesome, but **Cautley Crag** perhaps shows them at their most fearsome – dark cliffs of friable rock falling to a deep apron of scree. At the northern end, water cascades out of a hidden hanging valley, down a gash in the rock face, bouncing over a series of foaming steps for over 210m. The main fall is spectacular, and one of the highest in the country.

Ahead, the main path climbs steeply to the head of the valley, a strenuous pull that only relents as you broach the watershed of **Bowderdale Head**. Picking up pace, keep to the left of the boggy mass that sits atop the crest, soon passing the ruin of an abandoned sheep fold.

The view behind is now exchanged for the one ahead, an inviting prospect into the long, straight valley of Bowderdale, a lonely glen running north for more than 4½ miles (7.2km), before breaking free of the hills to join the River Lune. It is a fine walk indeed, but without the luxury of additional transport, it becomes a lengthy and demanding expedition.

As the ground begins to fall, break away from the path and make

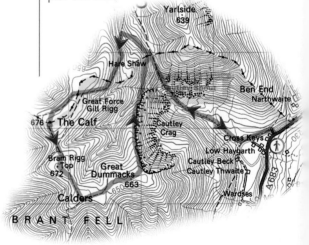

the best of the gradient to pick a slanting course across the untracked tussock, aiming to meet the path climbing out of Bowderdale along its western flank. Follow it back up above Hare Shaw, a memorable view opening ahead along the scalloped ridge of Cautley Crag and out along the valley to Baugh Fell.

Turning into a fold above Swere Gill, the path rises towards the central heights of the Howgill mass, eventually levelling onto an undulating plateau beside a couple of peaty pools. The scene ahead suddenly opens to reveal a distant skyline silhouetting the Lakeland peaks, while closer by is the long, curving ridge falling from Fell Head.

Beyond the pools, arc left to join another path, and where that later splits, keep left, rising gently past another pool to the top of **the Calf**, distinctly marked by a concrete trig column. Being the highest point of the Howgills, the views are truly impressive, and offer plenty of excuse to linger awhile.

Continuing past the trig, the path falls across an intervening saddle, rising over the only slightly lower mound of Bram Rigg Top. Perversely, the path ignores the challenge of locating the indistinct high spot, and instead makes a beeline for **Calders**, marked by a small pile of stones.

Now leaving the main trail, walk left on a grass path beside the fence above the head of the deep combe of Hobdale Beck. Reaching the top of Middle Tongue, the fence swings right. Turn with it, but after a few steps, bear away to the left on a faint trod. Where it shortly splits, take the left branch, which wanders on across the gently rising and almost featureless moor towards the barely perceptible summit of **Great Dummacks**.

Beyond the high spot, the way curves left to run as a more distinct but narrow path hugging the very rim of Cautley Crag's cliffs. The views are dramatic as the way winds along the edge, dropping toward the far end to cross Red Gill Beck above **Cautley Spout**. Carry on around an airy shoulder of rock, descending steeply to ford a second stream, Swere Gill.

Bowderdale Head and Yarlside from Cautley Crag

The excitement over, the path now runs easily across the slope of the grassy hill. After a few paces, a path drops very steeply beside the waterfalls and offers a direct descent. Less demanding, however, is to continue with the ongoing path, which angles gently down to Bowderdale Head. Meeting your outward path, turn right and follow it back to the Cross Keys Inn, enjoying a superb downhill romp that gives a fantastic view across to the falls.

WALK 7
Around Wandale Hill

Start	Rawthey Bridge (SD712979)
Distance	6 miles (9.7km)
Height gain	320m (1050ft)
Time	2hr30
Terrain	Moorland trods and tracks
OS map	Explorer OL19 – Howgill Fells & Upper Eden Valley
Refreshments	The Cross Keys Inn at Cautley, 1¼ miles (2km) south along A683
Toilets	None
Parking	Large lay-by at Rawthey Bridge

Many of the walks exploring the Howgill Fells call for at least one energetic and sustained ascent of the steep grassy slopes that buttress the high ground. But, as this undemanding route demonstrates, it is possible to experience a sense of remoteness and quietude without necessarily venturing onto the heights. This ramble perambulates the flanks of Wandale Hill, a southeastern outlier, taking in the two lovely valleys coursed by Wandale and Backside becks.

Follow the lane over **Rawthey Bridge** and, just past the narrow lane off to Uldale and Fell End, look for a stile on the left. Drop to a footbridge across Sally Beck and go left above it, passing its confluence with the River Rawthey. The way soon leads through a delightful coppiced wood, a rare treat in this part of the country, where extensive tracts of woodland are few and far between. ▶ Emerging into a field, carry on at its edge before returning through a small gate into the trees and dropping to another stream, **Wandale Beck**.

Note the condition of Wandale Beck, for you have to cross it here on the return, although high water is not a problem, since the ford can be avoided by an alternative

It is perhaps at its best in spring, when the leaves are barely formed and the understorey is carpeted with bluebell and ransom.

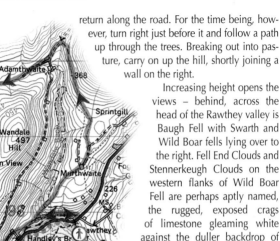

return along the road. For the time being, however, turn right just before it and follow a path up through the trees. Breaking out into pasture, carry on up the hill, shortly joining a wall on the right.

Increasing height opens the views – behind, across the head of the Rawthey valley is Baugh Fell with Swarth and Wild Boar fells lying over to the right. Fell End Clouds and Stennerkeugh Clouds on the western flanks of Wild Boar Fell are perhaps aptly named, the rugged, exposed crags of limestone gleaming white against the duller backdrop of the hillside. To the front is Harter Fell, while over on the left is Wandale Hill.

Leaving the field, walk down onto a track at **Murthwaite Farm** and swing left through a gate. At successive forks go first right and then later left, the way signed as a bridleway to Stonely Gill. A good track curves around the southwestern flank of Harter Fell, giving a superb view along Wandale to Adamthwaite Farm.

Shortly after passing above Adamthwaite Farm, watch out for a faint grass track branching off, which falls gently to the corner of a wall below, before turning down to the stream. Cross and climb to a narrow lane above.

The several place names ending in **'thwaite'** hereabouts hark back to the area's settlement by Scandinavians in the ninth and tenth centuries. The word comes from the Norse 'thveit', which describes a clearing made in the forest for cultivation, and implies that the woodland cover, now confined to narrow strips along the valleys, extended, even at that time, more extensively onto the open hillsides.

Go left for a few metres before splitting off onto a rising track, signed as a bridleway to Narthwaite. This contours the hillside above the farm then turns into the side valley of **Adamthwaite Sike**. After passing through a couple of gates by a large, modern farm shed, the track then swings in front of a gate by a large monolith. Bear left through the gate towards a small stone barn. Ignore the gate there, and instead walk on beside the wall, shortly dipping to a smaller gate and crossing a stream.

Rising beyond, the faint path accompanies the wall for a little distance before moving away. However, watch for it curving back to meet the stream and wall again. There swing left and pick your way across the waterlogged saddle between Wandale Hill and Grere Fell.

Crossing the watershed, curve left to pick up a trod above the confluence of Spen and Stockless gills, retaining your height around the northwestern flank of Wandale Hill. Becoming more pronounced, although still wet in places, the path continues above the biting fold of the valley. ▸

Becoming drier underfoot, the way begins to lose height, shortly passing above a remote farmstead,

Wandale Hill from Adamthwaite

Although there has been little strenuous climbing, you have penetrated a wonderfully remote corner of the Howgills, and the forbidding slopes of Kensgriff and Yarlside, deeply gashed by ravines holding the streams that drain them, add a wild dimension to the landscape.

Mountain View. Ignore the two gates there and continue beside the wall, the track narrowing to a rough path. Later, reaching a fork, bear right. Carry on down, passing through a couple of gates and ultimately reaching the farm at **Narthwaite**.

Through a gate on the left, pass into the yard, and cross to leave beside the farmhouse along its access track. After ¼ mile (400m), by a barn, the track swings right to the road.

If the ford at **Wandale Beck** (passed on the way out) appeared too deep to cross, you should remain with the track and then follow the lane back to the lay-by. Otherwise, abandon the track on the bend, and, through a gate, continue across a meadow to Wandale Beck. Retrace your outward route to Rawthey Bridge.

WALK 8
The River Rawthey's higher reaches

Start	Rawthey Bridge (SD712979)
Distance	5 miles (8km); onto Baugh Fell: 10½ miles (16.9km)
Height gain	260m (853ft); onto Baugh Fell: 610m (2001ft)
Time	2hr; onto Baugh Fell: 6hr
Terrain	Some rugged paths (clambering and trackless moorland on Baugh Fell)
OS map	Explorer OL19 – Howgill Fells & Upper Eden Valley
Refreshments	The Cross Keys Inn at Cautley, 1¼ miles (2km) south along A683
Toilets	None
Parking	Large lay-by at Rawthey Bridge

The main flow of the River Rawthey defines the southeastern boundary of the Howgill Fells, but its higher reaches curve back to separate the brooding mass of Baugh Fell from the nearby bulk of Swarth Fell Pike and Wild Boar Fell. These latter two hills are dealt with elsewhere in this volume, but Baugh Fell rather sits on its own, a great upturned pudding of a hill. Rising to 678m, it stands well apart from its neighbours and seems an inviting objective from afar. However, its spreading mass, largely cloaked by wet tussock and upland marsh, and a lack of trodden paths, make its ascent from any direction a demanding proposition.

Like much of its flanking slopes, the top is almost featureless – an expanse of weather-swept, sparse grass and moss, relieved only by a long wall that heads a rank of parallel enclosures draping the mountain's steep southern margin. It is a place to go for solitude and if you are moved to seek out its top, choose a day when the sky is clear, for it redeems itself with superb, far-reaching views of Swarth Fell Pike and the Howgills. On a fine day, although not technically difficult, it is a demanding and strenuous walk, but in poor visibility the summit has little merit and, unless you are experienced in such conditions and have good navigation skills, is best left alone.

The hill's undoubted gem, however, lies in the long valley of the upper River Rawthey, whose tributaries point a way to the summit. In its lower reaches the stream runs in an outstandingly pretty wooded clough, narrowing higher up past a succession of quietly impressive falls. For most folks, the exploration of this little-visited valley will be objective enough, returning across the more pastoral northern slopes of the valley.

Walk from the lay-by towards **Rawthey Bridge**, leaving the road just before it through a gate on the right. A rough, climbing track swings back parallel to the road, later levelling along the northwestern flank of Bluecaster, from where there is a good view across to Cautley Crag and its waterfall.

As the way twists to avoid a marshy depression, look for a waypost marking a junction with a grass path off to the left. It contours easily along the hillside, in time passing through a line of impressive shake holes. ◀ Farther along, tucked in a small gully on the right is the ruin of a lime kiln. The path eventually splits, the lower branch dropping to a footbridge across the river. However, for the moment, keep ahead on this bank up the narrowing valley.

These are caused by surface water washing overlying glacial clays into underground cracks and fissures within the underlying limestone.

Becoming more rugged, the path rises above the first of a succession of small but impressive waterfalls, partly concealed by trees crowding the narrow gorge. Through a gate, keep going along the valley side, passing a second smaller waterfall to reach Rawthey Gill Quarry.

Worked around the middle of the 19th century, the **rearing sandstone cliffs** provided both flags and building stone, which was then carted out of Uldale to the main road and down to Sedbergh. Little now remains of the enterprise other than the low ruins of several buildings that huddle amongst tips of abandoned spoil.

Keep with the higher path beyond the workings, which clambers across Slate Gill and continues up the valley towards another waterfall that blocks the gorge and marks a convenient far-point for the walk.

Extension onto Baugh Fell summit
Seasoned walkers seeking the summit of Baugh Fell can climb around to the right, bypassing the falls to continue up the valley. Further progress involves occasional

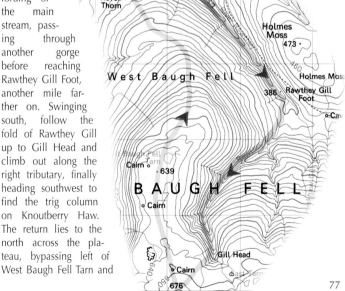

fording of the main stream, passing through another gorge before reaching Rawthey Gill Foot, another mile farther on. Swinging south, follow the fold of Rawthey Gill up to Gill Head and climb out along the right tributary, finally heading southwest to find the trig column on Knoutberry Haw. The return lies to the north across the plateau, bypassing left of West Baugh Fell Tarn and

Beyond West Baugh Fell Tarn to distant Wild Boar Fell

following the hill's indistinct northwestern snout down to Bluecaster. Drop off to the north and pick up your outward track back to the road.

Retrace your steps down the valley and cross the river on the footbridge. Climb away on a rising track at the edge of woodland, where you may see red squirrels. Some 20m after passing through a gate, bear off left through a gap in the accompanying wall. Pick your way between the trees, dropping to a footbridge over Needlehouse Gill. Walk on towards **Needle House**, joining a track that winds through the farmyard and on past the end of a barn, which sports an unusual projecting belfry, whose design was inspired by those adorning Scandinavian farms and was put up in the early 20th century to summon workers from the fields.

Beyond, pass through the rightmost of two gates. Continue along the field, leaving at the far right corner to continue at the head of more fields to New House Farm. Pass left of the building to pick up a rough track that rises to a ruined barn. Swing left through a gate and continue past a second barn. Paralleling the left wall, continue across more fields to another farm. Through the yard, keep going to the next farm, Wraygreen.

Pass through a gate in the field corner by the farmhouse and swing left, following the wall down to another gate. Keep going to the bottom-right corner of a final field to emerge onto a narrow lane. Go left and left again back to **Rawthey Bridge**.

WALK 9

Grisedale

Start	Garsdale Head (SD786919)
Distance	5 miles (8km)
Height gain	275m (902ft)
Time	2hr
Terrain	Some trackless moorland
OS map	Explorer OL19 – Howgill Fells & Upper Eden Valley
Refreshments	Moorcock Inn – 1 mile (1.6km) northeast of Garsdale Head
Toilets	None
Parking	Roadside parking off main road at Garsdale Head

This pleasant ramble wanders into the lonely glen of Grisedale. Although in places the moorland paths may not be apparent on the ground, the going is not difficult and, unless the mist is down, there are sufficient landmarks to keep you on the right track. In poor visibility a map and compass are essential.

Grisedale cuts a fold into the eastern slopes of Baugh Fell, and at one time supported 14 separate small farms and had both a Methodist chapel and Friends' Meeting House. But by the mid-1970s only one farm remained and many families had moved away. Barry Cockcroft's television documentary and book of the time perhaps prematurely dubbed it 'The Dale that Died', for life went on. The land is still grazed and Grisedale's solitude attracts escapees from the city rat race willing to restore the old cottages.

Garsdale Station, beside which the walk begins, was a busy junction connecting the Wensleydale Railway with the Settle and Carlisle line. The old railway cottages still stand, and were built to house employees when the through-line opened in 1876. However, the engine sheds, sidings and turntable, used to turn around engines that had double-headed trains out of Settle, have long since gone. A notable feature was a 43,000 gallon tank, which supplied troughs set in the track from which express trains could scoop water without stopping, to replenish the boiler after the long climb from the valleys below.

The great hill over to the left is Baugh Fell, while to the right, the ground rises to Lunds Fell. Behind, the railway winds around the flank of Widdale Fell before swinging north into the upper valley of the Ure, to cross the watershed into Eden.

From Garsdale Station walk down the lane to the main road and turn right. After 250m, at the crest of the hill, cross to a stile opposite a couple of cottages, from which a footpath is signed across the moor towards South Lunds. ◀ Crossing intervening boundaries, a discernible trod leads around the flank of a slight hill. It eventually falls, past the grassed spoil heaps of abandoned mine workings, towards cottages by a footbridge and railway level crossing at **South Lunds**.

Remaining on this side of the line, walk through a gate just beyond the footbridge. Bearing left, head out up the rough hillside grazing of South Lund Pasture. A developing faint path later draws beside a wall on the right, passing a gate and leading to a ladder stile near the far corner of the enclosure.

Having broached a layer of limestone, the going is now easier as you aim for a broad track, seen just right of ahead in the middle distance. Laid out before you is Grisedale, its small farms and cottages favouring the eastern slopes to enjoy the best of the sun. Later joining a wall on the left, the way develops to meet the track. Go left, zigzagging down to a gate above a farm, **East House**. However, before reaching the farmhouse, turn through a gate on the right, onto a track that leads to another small steading, **Fea Fow**. Approaching the cottage, look for a ladder stile on the left and skirt around the property. Carry on across the hillside towards a lone barn, and remain below the building as you cross a stream to a gate.

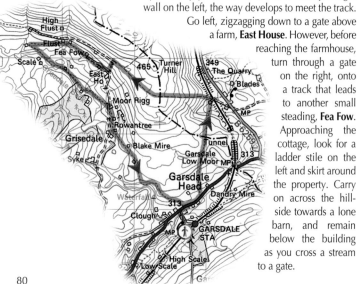

Ignoring a track falling to Scale, hold your height across the rough moor. Pass through a stile in a neglected lateral wall and keep going to a fingerpost by the corner of another wall. Gradually diverging from the boundary, maintain your heading to the ruin that was **Round Ing**, once the highest farm in the dale.

On the edge of Grisedale Common by East House Farm

Doubling back sharp left, follow the direction set by a signpost to Moor Rigg. Remain on the top of a bank, above the deepening gully of the infant Grisedale Beck, until, passing **Scale Farm**, the way drops to a bridge. ▶

Across the river, a wooded enclosure beside the farm is an old Quaker burial ground.

The onward route, however, stays on this bank, loosely following the stream towards the next settlement, **Reachey**. The fragment of building standing on the bluff above the opposite bank is all that remains of the Friends' Meeting House. Through a gate, bypass left of the cottage at Reachey. Cross its drive and briefly rejoin the river beyond, before rising up the bank to pass through a gate.

Joining the dale lane at **Moor Rigg**, walk past the house, and then immediately move off left across a meadow at a sign to Garsdale Head. Beyond a barn, continue in the next field towards a decaying building,

Rowantree. Cross a track to a gate beside the ruin and bear left, climbing to a waymarked gap in the wall ahead.

Keep going until you pass through a gate beside another cottage, **Blake Mire**, and then head right on a trod that curves above a steep-sided gully in which the river flows through Clough Force. The path shortly begins to fall towards the cottages at Garsdale Head, meeting the main road almost opposite the junction with the lane to Garsdale Station.

PART 2
MALLERSTANG

The Nab from Angerholme Pots (Walk 12)

WALK 10
High Seat

Start	B6270, ¼ mile (400m) west of national park boundary (SD808042)
Distance	4¼ miles (6.8km)
Height gain	215m (705ft)
Time	2hr30
Terrain	Indistinct upland trods
OS map	Explorer OL19 – Howgill Fells & Upper Eden Valley
Refreshments	None
Toilets	None
Parking	Roadside parking at start

Scraping in by a short head of just 1m, High Seat has the distinction of being the highest point overlooking Mallerstang, and is the fourth highest summit in the whole of the Yorkshire Dales. Notwithstanding all that, it can be readily climbed from the road at the top of the pass leading from the Eden Valley into Birk Dale. The route described here is a simple 'there-and-back' walk, but given a good day it can be extended, as time allows, further south along the wide ridge. This route is not recommended for inexperienced walkers in poor visibility, when a map and compass are essential.

Leave the B6270 some ¼ mile (400m) west of the national park boundary, opposite a bridleway sign pointing north to Rollinson Haggs and Hartley. An unmarked trod drops across a dip in the moor towards the steep northwestern flank of **High Pike Hill**.

After winding between a chain of impressive shake holes, it settles a course up the hill and, although barely visible in places, picks an ascent along the line of least resistance. Broaching a grassy plateau, the way then rises easily to a small hillock that resolves as the top.

High Seat now appears ahead on the skyline, still a goodly way off, but the views of the day are already with you. To the west across Mallerstang is a long line of hills – Little Fell, Wild Boar Fell and Swarth Fell. The market town of Kirkby Stephen lies in the base of the valley to the north, settled beneath the slopes of Nine Standards Rigg, while to the east and southeast, the notable points are Rogan's Seat and Great Shunner Fell respectively.

Beyond the summit cairn, the way falls easily onto a largely featureless expanse of short heather and sparse grass, broken by bare areas of sandy stone and occasional low islands of peat hag. Sheep, the odd grouse, and curlew and skylarks are likely to be your only company as the trod heads unerringly towards distant High Seat. In good visibility, navigation is not a problem, but when the cloud is down, care is necessary to remain on the right path. ▸

The flatness of the moor negates much of the panorama to the east, but the vista across the upper Eden Valley to Wild Boar Fell remains impressive.

Closer to High Seat the route skirts Lodge Hags and becomes increasingly boggy, the vague path often fragmenting in search of the driest route. Aim for a small cairn perched on a low band of exposed rock. The going, now

A broad featureless ridge takes the path from High Pike Hill to High Seat

The best views are to be had if you wander a little way to the west, where the ground falls away more steeply to reveal a dramatic prospect to the head of Mallerstang.

easier, continues onto **High Seat**, where a cairn marks the edge of the summit plateau. ◀

To the south, the broad, undulating line of hills meanders on for some 3½ miles (5.6km), to end at Lunds Fell, and having now gained the height, it is tempting to continue.

However, if you have not already arranged alternative transport, the only realistic return is back the same way. It is also prudent to keep an eye on the weather, since the lack of obvious paths on these hills can pose difficulties in route finding.

WALK 11
Pendragon Castle and
Little Fell

Start	Pendragon Castle (NY782026)
Distance	6 miles (9.7km)
Height gain	395m (1296ft)
Time	2hr30
Terrain	Moorland paths
OS map	Explorer OL19 – Howgill Fells & Upper Eden Valley
Refreshments	None
Toilets	None
Parking	Limited roadside parking by Pendragon Castle

Like parts of the Howgill Fells and Nidderdale, Mallerstang was left outside the Yorkshire Dales National Park, despite being topographically connected and possessed of a character and wild beauty that is equally captivating. That Mallerstang's watershed lies on the park boundary, and the valley offers some splendid walking, justifies its inclusion in this volume. A relatively easy climb leads onto the long western ridge, which further south culminates in Wild Boar Fell, and offers a splendid taste of the expansive views and sense of remoteness engendered by the high ground. It can be combined with the next walk, onto Wild Boar and Swarth fells, to create a longer and more demanding day out.

PENDRAGON CASTLE

The route begins from Pendragon, one of several Norman castles constructed along the Eden Valley as protection against the incursions of Scottish raiders, who wrought turmoil across the whole of the north for three centuries.

The original stone castle, built in 1173, is attributed to Hugh de Morville, but passed into the hands of the de Cliffords of Skipton in the early years of the 14th century. They bettered the defences, but even so, the fortifications were insufficient against the Scots, who burnt out the castle in 1341. Restored some 20 years later, it then remained in use for almost 200 years, before being destroyed again, although this time by an accidental fire.

It remained a ruin until the indefatigable Lady Anne inherited the Clifford estates in the mid-17th century. A woman of formidable spirit and untiring zeal, she invested her fortune in restoring many of her dilapidated properties, Pendragon amongst them. But after her death in 1676 it lapsed into permanent dereliction. Nevertheless, it still presents a romantically imposing sight – massively thick walls set upon a steep-sided mound, and defended by the river on one side and deep, dry moats on all others.

Tradition suggests an even earlier history for the place – the possible site of a Roman marching camp and, later, a Dark Ages citadel founded by Uther Pendragon, father of the legendary King Arthur. It is said that he died here with his warriors during a siege mounted by the Saxons, after they poisoned the water supply. The fact that there is not a single shred of documentary proof does nothing to lessen the appeal and endurance of the tales.

Pendragon Castle dates from the 12th century

Begin along the narrow lane leaving the B6259 beside **Pendragon Castle**. Follow it across the River Eden and wind gently uphill onto the open moor beyond. After

½ mile (800m), at a sharp right-hand bend, bear off left onto a bridleway. This rises across the rough tussock to a bridge across the Settle–Carlisle line, which runs below in a cutting to the mouth of a short tunnel, just to the north. Over the bridge, a vague track continues up the hillside, eventually bringing you to a gate in the accompanying wall.

Do not go through, but instead remain on the trod beside the wall. Increasing height reveals a fine view across the valley – behind is Mallerstang Edge, while to the north, the summit of Nine Standards Rigg peeps into view behind the flanks of High Pike Hill. Your objective, Little Fell, lies over to the left, although the summit will shortly be obscured by the intervening ground.

The path stays with the wall as it later curves around to the south, easily achieving height onto the broad shoulder of the hill. Reaching the crest, a panorama now opens to the Howgill Fells. Behind Harter Fell and Wandale Hill a succession of heights form the horizon – Green Bell, Randygill Top, Kensgriff and Yarlside – while below the ground falls across Kirkby Stephen Common to the expansive but unnamed tarn on Cook Mire. Its waters feed Scandal Beck, which cuts a circuitous course to meet the Eden downstream of Kirkby Stephen.

The wall, which has until now served as a guide, eventually swings away down the hill, leaving the faint path to continue its steady upward plod alone. After another ¼ mile (400m) a cairn suddenly springs into view, marking the edge of the wide and almost level summit plateau of **Little Fell**.

The spreading hill stretches on ahead to culminate in Wild Boar Fell, although the dramatic cliffs of the Nab vie for priority with the rather insignificant trig column marking the high point, which stands nearly ½ mile (800m) back to the right.

Maintain your southerly line across the top, beyond which the way loses height in an easy, loping descent to the corner of a wall at **Low Dolphinsty**.

If intending to continue onto Wild Boar Fell, climb ahead beside the wall to the next corner, **High Dolphinsty**, there meeting the path rising from Angerholme Pots. Otherwise, you can save yourself the effort of the ascent and bear off left on a grass path that cuts the corner across the slope of the hill. Although intermittently vague, your objective is clear – a distinct gravel path dropping from High Dolphinsty across the moor.

The climbing path to the Nab from Low Dolphinsty

Follow the path down the hill, later passing through a gate and carrying on to the ruins of an abandoned farmstead. Swing right beside a wall to dip across the often-dry bed of a stream, and walk to a junction with a track beside the railway. Doubling back, wind beneath a bridge and carry on down to a farm, **Hazelgill**. Go right and leave by its access track.

A short distance along, opposite a barn, turn off through the second of two small, adjacent gates on the left. Stride away with the wall on your left, negotiating successive gates and stiles from field to field. After passing over a stream, join a track that leads to Thrang Bridge. Do not cross – instead, continue downstream beside the Eden on this side.

Later, curving beneath a wooded bank, a track develops which leads to a farm. Bear left through the yard, bending right at a fork beyond as if to head back towards the river. However, almost immediately behind a barn, break away to the left across grass to a stile. The path soon rejoins the river through a particularly pretty section of woodland to reach another bridge.

Again remain on this bank and follow a track to cottages at **Shoregill**. Winding between the buildings, the track leads to a succession of white gates. After the first, choose the right-hand one of the pair, and then at the next pair, pass through the one on the left. Walk away at the field edge with the wall on your right.

Entering the third field, immediately cross a stile over a broken fence on the left and bear right on a rising grass path past a trio of birch trees to gain a low bank. The way continues ahead as a trod over stiles, shortly crossing a stream and climbing to an abandoned barn.

Passing it on the left, keep going over a stile to find a second stile on the right. Over that, bear left above the river before dropping to a gate and footbridge over a side stream. Skirt the perimeter of a paddock to leave at the far end behind a stable onto a lane. Turn right back to Pendragon Castle.

WALK 12

Wild Boar Fell and
Swarth Fell

Start	Cotegill Bridge on B6259 at Aisgill (SD773969)
Distance	8 miles (12.9km)
Height gain	535m (1755ft)
Time	3hr30
Terrain	Rugged, trackless moorland
OS map	Explorer OL19 – Howgill Fells & Upper Eden Valley
Refreshments	Moorcock Inn – 3 miles (4.8km) southeast of Cotegill Bridge
Toilets	None
Parking	Roadside parking by Cotegill Bridge

Wild Boar Fell is the culmination of the long, broad ridge of hill that defines the western margin of Mallerstang. Separated from its close neighbour, Swarth Fell, only by a shallow saddle, it naturally follows that the two hills should be combined in a single expedition. For those seeking a longer day, the ascent of Little Fell (Walk 11) makes a fine prelude, with several possibilities for a return – back onto the flanks of the hill via Angerholme Wold, across the slopes on the opposite side of the valley, or simply along the lane. However, the route is not recommended for inexperienced walkers in poor visibility, and the ability to use a map and compass is essential.

Wild Boar Fell takes its name, not unsurprisingly, from the fact that wild boar used to roam the valley. Tradition has it that the last one met its end here at the hands of Sir Richard Musgrave in the 16th century, and a tusk discovered interred in his tomb in Kirkby Stephen's church lends some credence to the tale, which has been immortalised in verse:

The giant with one stroke on his loins
Deprived the boar of life
Which gave a title to the hill
That ne'er will pass away,
For it is called Wild Boar Fell
E'en to this very day.

Follow the road north over **Cotegill Bridge** for nearly ½ mile (800m) to cross a bridge over Ais Gill by **Aisgill Farm**. Leave just beyond, through a gate on the left, from which a track climbs beneath a viaduct carrying the Settle–Carlisle railway.

It is worth a short detour beside the gully to look at the Ais Gill waterfalls above, but the onward route lies to the right, picking up the line of wall that runs more or less due north across the hillside. At first the going is rough and can be intermittently boggy, but later on improves as limestone develops underfoot.

THE SETTLE–CARLISLE RAILWAY LINE

Opened in 1876, the Settle–Carlisle line was a daring act by the Midland Railway to compete for the lucrative passenger and freight traffic along the already well-established east and west coast services to Glasgow and Edinburgh. The 72 mile (116km) route took six years to complete and cost over £3.5 million, exceeding the original estimate by over half.

It was an ambitious project, crossing some of the wildest landscape in England, and necessitating the building of 20 viaducts and 14 tunnels, as well as numerous bridges, cuttings and embankments. Although explosives and steam cranes were occasionally used, much of the gruelling work was undertaken by hand, and over 6000 men were employed along its length. Many of them were Irish immigrants, seeking escape from poverty and famine at home, but their lot was little better here. Accidents were frequent, and the men, often accompanied by their families, had to live in squalid shanty towns that moved along with the work, where insanitary conditions, disease and the appalling conditions of winter claimed untold lives.

At Ais Gill the line reaches its highest altitude, at 356m, as it crosses the watershed between the Ure and Eden valleys, having climbed over 200m in the 23 miles (37km) from Settle in the Ribble Valley. Known as the 'long drag', it was hard work for the most powerful locomotives, and even today, diesels hauling heavy freights are forced into a patient, rumbling crawl before reaching the top.

Encountering the first of a series of potholes, bear away from the wall and follow the line set by them. Many are quite spectacular, and are fenced, not necessarily to keep you out, for presumably you have the sense not to go poking about, but sheep don't, and the bouldery openings conceal significant drops into the netherworld. The path picks a line just east of them at the edge of the limestone across **Angerholme Wold**.

Reaching an expanse of cracked limestone pavement, the trod now swings left, rising more steeply towards the escarpment. Joining a path from below, follow a sloping rake that ascends through a nick to the corner of a wall at **High Dolphinsty**, where a path from the right brings the extended route of the previous walk from Little Fell.

Climbing onto the Nab from High Dolphinsty

Go left along the Scriddle ridge, the gradient gradually steepening to attain the top of **the Nab**, which is marked by a low cairn. Although not quite the highest point overlooking the valley, a distinction claimed by High Seat, 2¾ miles (4.4km) to the northeast, the vantage from the top of this craggy buttress affords the finest views along its length.

The Nab marks the edge of the Wild Boar Fell plateau, an extensive, roughly triangular cap of impermeable millstone grit. There is now a choice of objectives, both equally worthy of attention, and with the effort of ascent behind you, you may as well do both.

The high point of **Wild Boar Fell** is marked by a trig pillar standing some ½ mile (800m) to the southwest and is reached along a faint path. The ground to the west then falls away steeply across the bare scars of Ravenstonedale Common, revealing a superb panorama to the Howgill Fells. From the trig, cut back southeast across the plateau to the other high point above **Yoadcomb Scar**, where an intriguing group of 'stone men' stand sentinel above the cliffs.

The veritable forest of stone
men above Yoadcomb Scar

Like so many similar groups of cairns that dot the area, such as the Nine Standards and the Three Men of Gragareth, the origins of these **stone men** are lost in time. Perhaps they were built by quarrymen during idle moments, or by shepherds to serve as markers, but their distinctiveness compared to the more usual and readily constructed 'pile of stones' will perhaps forever remain a mystery.

The way continues over Swarth Fell, which lies almost due south, but a beeline is frustrated by the intervening deep gash of the head of Ais Gill. Therefore, remain on the northern side of the fence and follow it west from the 'stone men', above the steep slope of the Band.

In time the fence begins to curve to the south, dropping sharply to the corner of a wall on the broad saddle between the two hills. You can reach the same point from the summit trig point by striking southwest, picking up a trod that leads past the humps and hollows of old workings and eventually closes with the fence above the descent.

Cross the stile by the wall and carry on past a shallow tarn to ascend **Swarth Fell**. The rough path gradually steepens, abruptly levelling at a grassy shelf just below the top, where there is another smaller pool. Skirting its tip the path leaves the wall and climbs onto bare rocks to find the summit cairn, from which there is a grand view back to Wild Boar Fell.

Carry on parallel to the wall, gradually falling to another shallow saddle. As the wall ends, its line is continued by a fence, which guides you over the featureless top of **Swarth Fell Pike**. The way then begins to drop again, passing in succession two cairns located on the opposite side of the fence.

At the second cairn, as the ground ahead steepens towards White Birks Common, strike away to the left, picking a course across the trackless hillside towards **Aisgill Moor Cottages**, seen beside the road and railway, still a generous mile (1.6km) to the east.

In poor visibility there is nothing to guide you, and the ability to use map and compass is essential. A direct bearing is not the ideal course, as the deepening gully of Smithy Gill lies in the way. You should, therefore, arc slightly to the south, to end up along Stubbing Rigg, a route that follows the line of the national park boundary marked on the Ordnance Survey map down to the road. The aim is to find a gate off the hillside opposite a track just south of the cottages. Turn left along the road and walk back to Cotegill Bridge.

PART 3
SWALEDALE AND
ARKENGARTHDALE

One of the cavernous Buttertubs (Walk 22)

WALK 13

*Apedale and
Harkerside Moor*

Start	Grinton – Redmire road, 1½ miles (2.4km) south of Grinton (SE038963)
Distance	9¾ miles (15.7km)
Height gain	440m (1444ft)
Time	4hr
Terrain	Moorland paths and tracks
OS map	Explorer OL30 – Yorkshire Dales (Northern & Central Areas)
Refreshments	Bridge Inn at Grinton
Toilets	At Grinton
Parking	Roadside parking area at start
Note	Dogs are not allowed on Open Access land away from rights of way

Straddling the watershed between Wensleydale and Swaledale, this walk perambulates the upper moorland surrounding High Carl. Although unremarkable in itself, the hill is gouged by two secluded valleys that once reverberated to the tumultuous din of lead mining, but which now lie silent, save for the calls of upland birds. Far-reaching vistas reveal different facets of this fascinating landscape, while the mystery of an ancient earthwork gives further food for thought.

Leave the parking area on a developing path that rises southwest across rabbit-nibbled turf and heather onto **Greets Hill**. Exchanging backward glances of Swaledale for a view into Wensleydale, pass through a gate and continue down the other side to a crossing of tracks at **Dent's Houses**. Turn right and head into **Apedale**, which, like the hill above, was heavily worked for its lead during the 19th century.

Remain on the main path as the valley narrows, climbing more steeply onto the open moor above its head. Breasting the watershed, the track doglegs past more mine shafts to a gate in a boundary fence, and continues beyond in a loping descent, revealing a grand panorama into the middle reaches of Swaledale, past Gunnerside towards Muker.

Less than half a mile's walking (800m) brings you to a great heap of stones beside the path, yet another shaft. In the 19th century prospecting relied upon at least as much luck as science, and from its name, **Morley's Folly**, it seems that this was one venture where fortune failed. It does, however, serve to mark the point at which the bridlepath, shown on the Ordnance Survey map but not evident on the ground, leaves the track.

An impressive lime kiln on Harkerside Moor

A clearer alternative is to continue with the main track for a further ¼ mile (400m) to a junction by more extensive workings. Turn right, shortly crossing Birks Gill.

The ongoing track undulates easily across the steepening northern flank of High Carl, where the view opens down the valley towards Reeth and Fremington Edge. The layered nature of the geology is revealed in the profile of the valley, where bands of harder limestone stand out in a series of stepped terraces falling through layers of underlying softer sandstones.

101

As the slope of the hill increases below, the way broaches the limestone and comes upon a monumental lime kiln.

Fed at the top from a small quarry, the burnt lime was raked out through the arched opening at the base of the **lime kiln**. Size alone suggests that this was a fairly large-scale enterprise, and notice too the remains of rails on which tubs of rock and fuel – poor-grade coal known as culm, and dug from thins seams found on the higher moors – were run to charge it. For convenience, the outer structure is of the very same stone it was built to roast, but sandstone had to be brought from elsewhere to provide a lining to prevent its self-destruction. The burnt lime was used as fertiliser in the valley fields, but huge quantities were also required to produce building mortar for use at the mine and processing floors.

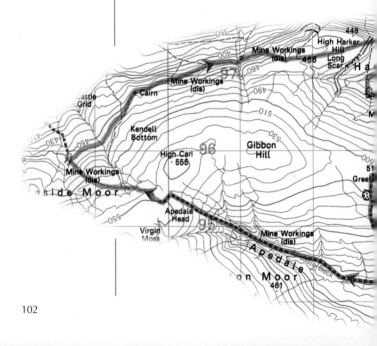

The way then falls, eventually crossing **Browna Gill**. Signed to Grinton, the onward track continues past a shooting hut to a fork. Bear right, winding around the fringe of the Harker workings onto the broad top of High Harker Hill.

A lone shooting hut stands by Browna Gill

Losing sight of Swaledale, a vista now opens into the deepening fold of Grovebeck. Dropping off the eastern edge of the plateau, the track cuts through an impressive wall of stone rubble, strategically following the line of the escarpment and protected by the deep ditch of an earthwork on its lower side.

As the gradient eases, a small pile of stones indicates a crossing path. To the right, it strikes a beeline across the heather towards a stone hut and the tips of the **Grovebeck** lead mine. However, the path is faint, and you can instead remain with the track, which continues for a

EARTHWORKS

The route passes one of several earthworks in the area, which together create a line of defence below the confluence of Arkengarthdale and Swaledale. They were traditionally interpreted as Celtic tribal boundaries, dating to the Iron Age, that is, around 500BC. However, it is now suggested that they may not have been built until after the departure of the Roman garrisons, at the beginning of the fifth century, and in fact served as a boundary between the native British and the new wave of invaders, the Anglo-Saxons. Indeed, according to a sixth-century Welsh ballad, the Gododdin, whose kingdom was centred on the eastern Scottish border, were defeated by the Anglians in a great battle nearby at Catraeth, present-day Catterick.

further ¼ mile (400m) to a junction. Turn right and follow a track back around the side of the hill to meet the mapped bridleway by a bridge spanning Grovebeck Gill. After climbing to the hut, the track swings left and runs easily for another mile (1.6km) to the Grinton road. The parking area is then a short distance up the hill.

Over to the left, tucked within Cogden Gill, is the **Grinton smelt mill**, which was built around 1820. The lower building housed the furnaces while the other served to store the peat used as fuel. The structure climbing straight up the hill behind was a flue, drawing off the poisonous gasses released in the smelting process. But there was other industry too, revealed in the three arches set higher up. They are the remains of a large lime kiln, one of six that once stood on the hill.

WALK 14
Grinton and Maiden Castle

Start	Grinton (SE046984)
Distance	4¾ miles (7.6km)
Height gain	210m (689ft)
Time	2hr
Terrain	Moorland and riverside paths
OS map	Explorer OL30 – Yorkshire Dales (Northern & Central Areas)
Refreshments	Bridge Inn at Grinton
Toilets	At Grinton
Parking	Roadside parking in village

Yorkshire's Maiden Castle might not be as imposing or famous as the one just outside Dorchester in Dorset, but its unusual design and location pose a much bigger mystery. It stands on the flanks of Harker Hill, overlooking the Swale, and is easily reached by this ramble from Grinton, which makes a pleasant return along the riverbank.

From the Bridge Inn by the church, follow the lane south towards Leyburn. Some 50m beyond the junction, turn off along a track between cottages on the right to the field behind. Strike to a narrow gate at the far side and, negotiating a marshy stream, swing up the field edge beside it. Leaving the top of the next field by a barn, keep ahead to join a grass path from the left, now climbing onto the open moor.

Meeting an intersecting path, bear right, before long passing through a gate. Where the right-hand wall later kicks away, contour across the slope along a clear trod. Harker Hill rises on your left and across the valley is Calver Hill. ▶ Encountering a rough track by the corner of a wall, drop right, looking for a broad grass path a few

On the hillside west of Reeth, accentuated in a late afternoon sun, are lynchets, the banks of ancient cultivation terraces resulting from ploughing strips across the hillside.

metres along on the left. It undulates easily across the slant of the hill, shortly crossing a line of shooting butts. A little way beyond, as the track then curves left towards High Harker Hill, abandon it for a narrow but distinct trod ahead through the heather.

Another 300m brings you above the parallel collapsed walls that formed an avenue to **Maiden Castle**, the path remaining high above the earthwork and giving an encompassing view of the site. Carry on until you have passed its western end, when you will then find a path that drops back to it.

MAIDEN CASTLE

Former antiquarians regarded Maiden Castle as a Bronze or Iron Age fortification, associating it with the many linear earthworks to be found in this part of the valley. More recent thinking dates it to the Iron Age period, before the Roman conquest, and has posed alternative theories as to its purpose, although no one really knows for sure why it was built.

The oblate enclosure is poorly placed for a defensive structure, as it is directly overlooked by the higher ground to the south, by which you made your approach. Also, hill forts often have a staggered entrance, designed to confuse and hinder unwanted visitors, but this is approached by a walled processional walk leading to a simple gateway. Some authorities have likened it to the 'banjo' stock enclosures found in the south, but this perhaps served a ceremonial function, particularly as there are a number of burial tumuli in the area. One was held 'to contain an iron chest filled with riches', but like many other fabled treasure troves, has never been proved. Whatever, the monument was important to its people, representing a huge investment in labour, and requiring a well-organised and resourceful society to undertake the task.

Having taken your fill and formulated your own theory as to Maiden Castle's purpose, continue with the path down the hill beyond its lower western tip, arcing left to meet the lane below. Go left for 75m to a sign indicating a crossing bridleway, and double back down the bracken-cloaked hillside to a gate near the bottom corner of the enclosure. Carry on to **Stubbin Farm**, passing left of the longhouse and on along a short walled track behind.

Turn right along a terrace, which soon falls to a gate beside the **River Swale**. The way continues pleasantly beside the bank, speckled with flowers and lined with sycamore and alder, a type of wood that was used, amongst other things, for making clogs. Entering the corner of a large pasture, a bridge comes into view ahead.

Maiden Castle commands a fine view to Fremington Edge

Although obviously a suspension bridge, it is curiously known as **Reeth Swing Bridge**, perhaps because it sways when you walk across. The present structure replaces the original bridge, which was built in 1920, but carried away when struck by a passing tree during a flood in September 2000.

Soon, at a clump of broken trees, the path moves away from the river, cutting to a gate in the far-right corner. Carry on beside a wall, maintaining the same course beyond its end to meet a former bank of the river. Through a couple of gates, an old green way wanders on for another ½ mile (800m), finally ending onto a lane by **Swale Hall**. Follow it left back to Grinton.

'CATHEDRAL OF THE DALES'

St Andrew's is not the only church to claim the title 'Cathedral of the Dales', but its parish was certainly once the largest and, until the parish of Muker was formed in 1580, stretched the full length of Swaledale to the Westmorland border, some 17 miles (27km) away. This partly accounts for the extensive graveyard, needed to accommodate those carried down in wicker baskets for burial here, a journey that sometimes took three days. There was already a Christian tradition when William de Ghent raised the first stone church soon after the Conquest, endowing it and the surrounding lands to St Mary's Priory at Bridlington. The church was rebuilt in the 14th century, and only the font and a round-headed window, set high in the west wall but blocked by the later tower, remain from those early days. An interesting feature is a medieval leper's squint hole, enabling the afflicted to watch the ceremony at the high altar without risk of infecting the rest of the villagers.

WALK 15

Fremington Edge

Start	Reeth (SE038992)
Distance	7¼ miles (11.7km)
Height gain	415m (1362ft)
Time	3hr
Terrain	Moorland and riverside paths
OS map	Explorer OL30 – Yorkshire Dales (Northern & Central Areas)
Refreshments	Pubs and cafés in Reeth
Toilets	At Reeth
Parking	Around village green (honesty box)
Note	Dogs are not allowed on Open Access land away from rights of way

Fremington Edge rises abruptly behind the attractive town of Reeth, but an old track provides a pleasant and relatively undemanding way onto the top. There are spectacular views as the route then follows the lip of the scar to Fell End, before dropping to the foot of Slei Gill. The return meanders through the pasture and woodland bordering Arkle Beck, offering a walk of great contrasts at any time of the year. For a longer day, the route can be combined with Walk 16 into Slei Gill.

Begin from the upper-right corner of the green by **Ivy Cottage Tearoom**. Walk up past Arkleside Country Guest House and turn down the hill. At the bottom, keep ahead along a short track to the river and follow it downstream to **Reeth Bridge**. Double back over it across Arkle Beck, but as the road then swings right, leave through a way-marked gate on the left. Bear right to a second gate and maintain your line across the adjacent meadow to a squeeze stile, partway along the upper wall. Follow the wall right, shortly emerging onto a narrow tarmac track.

The Black Bull Hotel in Reeth

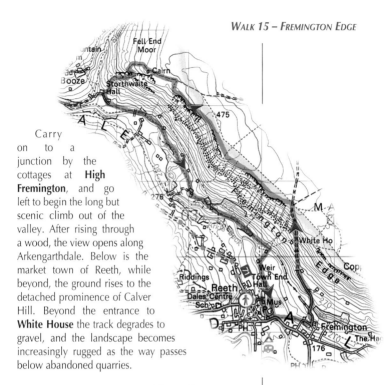

Carry on to a junction by the cottages at **High Fremington**, and go left to begin the long but scenic climb out of the valley. After rising through a wood, the view opens along Arkengarthdale. Below is the market town of Reeth, while beyond, the ground rises to the detached prominence of Calver Hill. Beyond the entrance to **White House** the track degrades to gravel, and the landscape becomes increasingly rugged as the way passes below abandoned quarries.

> The stone obtained from the cliffs was **chert,** a very hard type of flint. When ground to a fine powder it was used in the manufacture of china, but flags were also cut from it, and it is said that stone from here was used to pave the streets of Paris.

The track finally levels to a gate in a wall running the length of the scar. The right of way follows its opposite side, but misses the stunning views along the valley. So instead, turn off left just before the gate, finding a trod that passes between the low heaps of old workings to run along the lip of **Fremington Edge**.

Crossing occasional boundaries, the way continues for about a mile (1.6km), eventually scaling a ladder stile. Beyond, the path begins to lose height, shortly meeting a trod climbing out of the valley. Bear right towards the spoil from more mineshafts, joining a bridleway that has crossed the moors from Hurst.

Follow it left gently down the hill, later zigzagging more steeply through the workings and running out beside a deep gully. Towards the far end of the gully, turn through a gate in the left-hand wall and head straight down the field. Funnelled to a walled track at the bottom, the way ends at a junction by a creeper-clad cottage at **Storthwaite Hall**.

From here, you have the option of extending the walk into Slei Gill and Langthwaite. In which case, go right, crossing a footbridge spanning the stream and climbing to a second junction. There turn right again and pick up the instructions given in Walk 16.

The way back to Reeth, however, lies to the left. Where the track shortly ends at another cottage, walk through the yard and continue beyond, meeting the river and the linking path from Langthwaite towards the end of the second meadow.

Passing a bridge across the river, the path almost immediately divides. If the river has been high, the best option would be to take the bridlepath signed to the left, which rises to **Heggs House**. Pass behind the buildings and through a gate before then veering right to follow a neglected wall. The path contours the valley side for a mile (1.6km) before reuniting with the lower path beyond **Castle Farm**.

The right fork, signed to Reeth, has its charms however, and passes through a delightful wood where damp patches harbour a remarkable assortment of wild flowers.

Among the **wildflowers** you might spot are ragged robin, forget-me-not, orchid, speedwell, and the 'Germoline plant' – my own name for meadowsweet, whose tiny feather flower heads emit a scent reminiscent of the thick pink salve liberally applied as a childhood cure-all for cuts, stings and burns. The name is, in fact, a corruption of medesweete, as it was used to flavour mead, and as an infusion, prescribed to ease pain and reduce fever. Science has proved the basis of many folk medicines, and meadowsweet is now known to contain compounds similar to those found in aspirin.

Breaking from the trees, bear away from the river around the base of the higher ground to avoid a marshy area. Picking up a streambed, follow it to a stile and then cross back to the left bank. Where the river shortly swings right, the path rises ahead towards **Castle Farm**.

Pass left of the cottage and then, in the small field behind, cross to an irregular wall opposite. Clamber through a broken gap and carry on to a squeeze stile, beyond which the way gently falls beside a wall, and later, past an abandoned farmstead. Before long the trail draws closer to the river and joins the alternative bridle path.

Swaledale sheep in upper Arkengarthdale

Passing into more trees, bear left at a fork to climb above the river once more. Eventually leaving the wood behind, continue beside an undulating wall for ½ mile (800m). Reaching a field gate on the right, head down past a barn. Entering the third field, turn left by the wall and carry on through a squeeze gate at the far end. Later, faced with two gates, pass through the one on the left and keep going, ultimately returning to the road by Reeth Bridge.

WALK 16

Slei Gill

Start	Langthwaite (NZ005023)
Distance	5¾ miles (9.3km)
Height gain	320m (1050ft)
Time	2hr30
Terrain	Rough paths and moorland tracks
OS map	Explorer OL30 – Yorkshire Dales (Northern & Central Areas)
Refreshments	The Red Lion in Langthwaite
Toilets	At Langthwaite
Parking	Car park on main lane, just south of Langthwaite (pay and display)
Note	Dogs are not allowed on Open Access land away from rights of way

The picturesque mining village of Langthwaite makes a great base for a number of walks. This one ventures into the intimate side-valley of Slei Gill, where there is plenty to see in the relics of its former industry. The return winds across empty moors where the clear tracks don't always correspond to mapped paths. This route can readily be tacked on to that from Reeth along Fremington Edge to make a longer ramble (see Walk 15), and as there is refreshment at either end, it doesn't really matter where you start. This route is not recommended for inexperienced walkers in poor visibility, and the ability to use a map and compass is essential.

From the car park follow the road right and then go right again, dropping across the bridge into old **Langthwaite**. The Red Lion stands on the left, but you should turn right to find a track beside Arkle Beck. After later stepping back behind meadows, the track rises to a fork.

If extending the walk to include Fremington Edge, Reeth is to the right, the path dropping back to the river

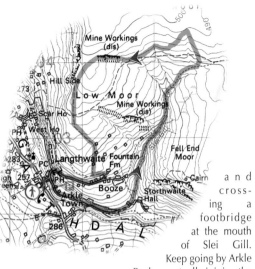

and crossing a footbridge at the mouth of Slei Gill. Keep going by Arkle Beck, eventually joining the bridlepath from **Storthwaite Hall**. The ongoing instructions are to be found in Walk 15.

The Slei Gill circuit, however, takes the left branch, soon reaching another junction, where the return path from Reeth along Fremington Edge joins from the right. Keep going towards the deep fold of **Slei Gill**, passing a fork to reach a hurdle gate in the wall ahead. A grass path continues into the narrowing confines of the valley above the stream.

'HUSHES' AND 'ADITS'

One of the startling features of the valley is the succession of deep gullies, or hushes, that break the steep slopes on both sides. In the early days, lead ore could readily be found outcropping on the surface and merely had to be dug out. 'Hushing' was an effective way of getting rid of the over-blanket of vegetation and rubble, and involved a convenient stream being dammed above the vein and then released in a stripping torrent. Once the underlying ore had been dug out, the process was repeated to remove the waste, and the gully progressively deepened until either the vein was worked out, or forced the miners underground.

Further up the path, water gushes from a narrow slit cut into the rock face. Many 'adits', horizontal tunnels as distinct from vertical shafts, were dug to provide easy access to the workings, enabling tubs of ore simply to be pushed out of the mine rather than hoisted upwards. Others like this were dug to drain the workings, since accumulating water was an ever-present problem, and would otherwise need to be pumped out to prevent flooding.

The path leads up the valley, eventually reaching a splay of streams at its head, where there is a stone ruin. Pass it to the right, climbing the bank behind. At the top, go right along the edge to a small cairn, there winding sharp left and then right to find a narrow trod leading away through the heather and bilberry, keeping the easternmost tributary stream to your right.

At first glance, the ruin has the appearance of a lime kiln, but closer inspection suggests a very different purpose. In fact, it housed a **water wheel,** the leat tapping the stream higher up the hillside and now buried beneath the collapsed spoil heap behind. However, the exit arch for the tailrace is still clearly visible. Power from the wheel would have been transmitted through a system of belts and drive shafts to the pit-heads, where it was used to operate winding gear or pumping equipment.

After some 400m, as the gradient eases, watch for the trod curving from the stream and rising onto a low bank. Walk forward across the flat depression behind and climb again to join a developing track, which leads up to meet the bend of another track. Follow it ahead, more or less north for ¼ mile (400m) to a junction and go left, in time passing a large hut.

The track then shortly swings right, winding up through a worked-out gully that crests amongst a rash of abandoned pits, which exploited the rich **Windegg** and **White Gang** veins. Reaching a hairpin bend, turn off left along a lesser track, which runs south in gentle descent for another ½ mile (800m), looking out across Arkengarthdale.

In the valley below is the 18th-century **CB Inn,** named for Charles Bathurst, whose family settled here when Dr John Bathurst, personal physician to Oliver Cromwell, bought the manor in 1656. With the manor, Dr John acquired its tenants, and by all accounts was not impressed with their attitude, for at one point he reputedly threatened to have them all shipped out to the colonies if they didn't agree his terms. His real interest in the valley was its lead, and the veins of ore in the Moulds mines on the opposite hillside were said to be 'seven fathoms high and a yard broad', and yielded him profits of £1000 per year, a tidy sum in those days.

Ignore a fork, shortly passing the corner of a wall, but as the track then swings left at a waypost, cut right to a gate and stile tucked into the corner. Accompany the wall down, soon joining forces with a grass track, but where that later turns through a gate, keep ahead into the narrowing field bottom.

Beyond a gate, as the walls open out, bear left at a waypost down a rough path. Meeting a track by the ruin of a small farm, go right and right again, following the track all the way down the hill back into Langthwaite.

Across the Langthwaite to the Charles Bathurst lead mines on Moulds Moor

WALK 17
Whaw to Dale Head

Start	Whaw Bridge (NY980042)
Distance	4½ miles (7.2km)
Height gain	220m (722ft)
Time	2hr
Terrain	Field trods and trackless moorland
OS map	Explorer OL30 – Yorkshire Dales (Northern & Central Areas)
Refreshments	The Charles Bathurst Inn near Langthwaite
Toilets	At Langthwaite
Parking	Limited roadside parking on main lane outside Whaw

Whaw is the highest settlement of Arkengarthdale, the road climbing beyond across empty moor to Tan Hill and Stainmore. It is an area little frequented by walkers, but those who do venture this far will discover a wild beauty in the rough meadows and upland grazing that rise around the head of the valley. In consequence, the paths upon the ground are at best vague, and, particularly in poor visibility, the ability to use a map and compass is necessary. Although there are fewer narrow gap stiles to negotiate than on some walks, most of the gates are of the non-opening kind.

From the junction, follow the narrow lane down to the river, crossing the bridge into **Whaw**. Swing left though the hamlet, passing the former chapel.

> The **chapel** was built in 1840 at a cost of £200 and, not unsurprisingly, had one of the smallest congregations of Swaledale's nine Methodist chapels, with only 14 members recorded in 1865. In 1964 it was converted into a dwelling.

Parting from the stream, the lane rises at the foot of a steep bank above a succession of riverside meadows. As it later bends to climb beside a wooded gully, bear off along a gated track to Low Faggergill Cottage and Hill Top Farm. Reaching an open green at **Low Faggergill**, keep left and then swing in front of the cottage to a gate.

Walk up beside the building and immediately turn through a second gate, doubling back behind the cottage. Bear right on a trod across the meadow to a stile beside a gate. A fine view opens into the upper reaches of Arkle Beck as you maintain the line to another gate. Then, keeping slightly right, the way chooses the high ground, leading to a stile in the far corner.

> Amongst the early summer flowers livening the grass is **yellow rattle**, so named because of the sound produced when the ripe seedpods are shaken, and in some places this was taken as the time to begin hay-making. The plant is unusual in that it is partly parasitic, the roots tapping into those of the surrounding grass to gain some of its nourishment.

Now bear left, passing the end of a short wall to carry on across rougher pastures to **Hill Top Farm**. A track

Hill Top Farm and the upper reaches of Arkengarthdale

119

leads into the yard and past the front of the farmhouse to a gate. Keep the same direction for another ¼ mile (400m) to the next farm, Dale Head. Walk through a gate into the yard, keep left beside the farmhouse and turn right past a barn to leave by another gate. The onward track climbs away, shortly curving up to the final farm of the valley, **Ravens Park**.

Entering the farm, stay ahead on an enclosed grass track in front of the farmhouse, and pass out through a gate at the end onto the open upland grazing. Stay beside the wall for ½ mile (800m), at which point it turns away down the hill. The line of the path, however, continues ahead, so set a course for the right-hand edge of the flat-topped hill in the middle distance, **Kitely Hill**.

The prominent spoil tips mark the site of the Faggergill Lead Mines, which managed to keep going into the early decades of the 20th century.

The way falls gently over rough tussock into a shallow fold, which cups the stream draining Faggergill Moor over to the left. ◄

You are aiming to meet the stream at a small bridge, over which is a gate. Climb away paralleling the left wall to another gate at the top and pursue the same line beyond, passing the rounded corner of a wall to join a gravel track. Follow it down, ultimately meeting a narrow lane at **Seal Houses**.

Go right past a large barn, but then, just before the farmhouse, leave through a squeeze stile on the left. Cross to a narrow gate opposite and, bearing left, continue from field to field down the hillside to a wood. The ongoing path zigzags steeply through the trees, emerging into a lawned garden beside the former Methodist chapel. Double back to a ladder stile and follow the drive out to the lane near the bridge, retracing your outward steps to your car.

WALK 18
Old Gang and Surrender

Start	Surrender Bridge (SD989998)
Distance	5½ miles (8.9km)
Height gain	265m (869ft)
Time	2hr15
Terrain	Moorland tracks
OS map	Explorer OL30 – Yorkshire Dales (Northern & Central Areas)
Refreshments	The Punch Bowl Inn at Low Row
Toilets	None
Parking	Lay-by at Surrender Bridge

Although lead ore was mined in many places throughout the Dales, the greatest concentration of the industry was on the hillsides enclosing Swaledale. The scars of old workings and tips abound, but nowhere are the remains of the buildings associated with them more impressive than here along Old Gang Beck, where there were two large smelt mills. The walk follows the valley to its head, returning over Great Pinseat, one of the highest places in the Dales where mines were dug.

SURRENDER MILL

Built in 1840 on the site of an earlier smelt house, Surrender Mill stands on a broad shelf above the stream. The main building housed a roasting oven and four separate hearths, in which the ore was reduced to metal and cast into 'pigs'. Between the smelting hearths was a pit, over which a water wheel was slung. This drove bellows that blasted air to raise the temperature of the furnace fires, and provide oxygen to complete the chemical process.

The fumes, a mixture of sulphur dioxide, carbon monoxide and vaporised lead, had to be drawn off, but on a windless day a simple chimney merely left the deadly cloud hanging over the site and, more importantly from the owner's point of view, lost valuable lead. To combat this, the gases were extracted through a long flue, which here ran for almost ½ mile (800m) to a chimney sited on top of the hill. As the gases cooled during their passage, the lead condensed within the flue and, periodically, small boys were given the unenviable task of crawling inside to scrape out the deposits for reprocessing.

The furnaces demanded constant supplies of fuel, which was plentiful in the form of the peat blanketing the moors above. Once cut and brought down, it was stored in the long peat house, whose ruins stand on the higher ground just to the northeast. The side walls consisted merely of pillars to support a thatched roof, allowing air to circulate and thus dry out the peat for burning.

The ash and slag from the hearths was simply dumped along the riverbank, polluting the stream and creating an almost concrete-like mass on which nothing will now grow.

The Old Gang smelt mill

You can be forgiven for not even starting this walk, for the Surrender Mill is overlooked from the parking area and begs immediate investigation.

With luck, there is still enough left of the day to explore further, for there is plenty more to see higher up the valley. Return to the road and continue upstream along the broad

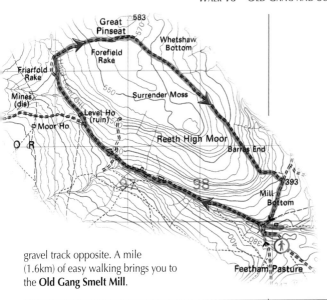

gravel track opposite. A mile (1.6km) of easy walking brings you to the **Old Gang Smelt Mill**.

THE OLD GANG SMELT MILL

The ruins here are even more extensive than those at Surrender, the largest building housing the smelting hearths. Behind is a complex arrangement of ducts drawing the fumes off to the flue, which climbed almost to the top of the hill, 150m above. The tall chimney beside the track rose from a separate furnace, in which the ore was given a preliminary roasting prior to the final smelting.

Further on, below the track, is a row of old bunkers, or bouse teems, and a dressing floor, where ore from the mines was stored, broken down and prepared for smelting, while just beyond there is a small holding reservoir. Several entrances to the levels are also to be seen, most now pouring out water from the flooded mines deep within the hill.

The peat store is not immediately obvious, but there is a good view back to it as you climb beyond the site. The largest in the area, it was almost 120m long, and reputed to be capable of storing enough peat to fire the furnaces for three years.

Continue with the main track up the valley for a further ½ mile (800m), eventually passing through a gate to **Level House Bridge**. Instead of crossing, bear off on a

Along the Coast to Coast to
Level House Bridge

narrower path into the more intimate valley of **Flincher Gill**. ▶ Higher up, beside the path, twin entrances to one of the levels have been restored, the tunnels sloping steeply into the bowels of the hill. Inviting though they may look, especially if you have a torch in your pack, such places are full of danger, and definitely not for the inexperienced.

Passing through a gate a little further on, the track curves to the right, climbing gently along a strip of bare desolation all the way to the top of **Great Pinseat**. ▶ Cairns mark the path to the crest of the hill, although the actual summit then lies a short distance further north on the line of a parallel wall.

Beyond the crest the path again arcs to the right, running in a pleasant, if uneventful, grassy descent high above the deepening fold of Bleaberry Gill. Towards the end, the way falls more steeply past another rash of workings, finally winding out to meet a lane.

Surrender Bridge lies ½ mile (800m) to the right; remember to look out for the flue from the smelt mill as it passes beneath the road.

The scars of mining line the way and extend across the higher moor, tracing the courses of the veins of ore deep beneath the ground.

The raw wound of the workings can be traced in an almost unbroken line, across the moors, that stretches for almost 8 miles (12.9km), from Swinner Gill all the way to Hurst, cutting straight through the valleys of Gunnerside, Mill Gill and Arkle Beck.

WALK 19

*Beside the River Swale
from Gunnerside*

Start	Gunnerside (SD950982)
Distance	4½ miles (7.2km)
Height gain	175m (574ft)
Time	1hr45
Terrain	Field trods and tracks
OS map	Explorer OL30 – Yorkshire Dales (Northern & Central Areas)
Refreshments	The King's Head and Ghyllfoot Tearoom in Gunnerside
Toilets	Beside the King's Head
Parking	In village centre near bridge

A short pull at the start takes this enjoyable walk onto the middle grazing pastures and woodland of the valley side, giving some splendid views over the gently meandering Swale below. The return is beside the river, along an old lane that once served the valley, but which has now lapsed into retirement as a delightful track.

Crossing the bridge, follow the lane past the pub and through the village. At **Town End**, bear off left up a steep, gated drive, abandoning this where it subsequently bends for an old, intermittently walled track that rises ahead. After crossing a stream, Stanley Gill, the track then passes the ruin of a pair of miners' cottages commanding an idyllic outlook over the valley.

Not far beyond, the walls step back and the track swings up towards a farm, **Heights**. However, leave on the bend, going forward across a stream to a stile. The way continues ahead below the farm buildings, across the springy turf of a series of pastures before entering **Rowleth Wood**.

A rugged path winds through the trees that cloak the steep slope – rowan, hazel, birch, blackthorn, hawthorn and ash, overshadowed here and there by larger sycamores. Breaking out beyond, carry on across more fields, the path drawing towards the upper wall and shortly arriving at **Smarber Farm**. Leave through a gate on the left into the yard and turn right to follow the track out. As the track swings left, go right across a stream to a field gate in the corner by a cottage.

A grass track guides you in a gradual descent across the gradient of the hill, eventually passing through a gate to meet the

The old green lane out of Gunnerside

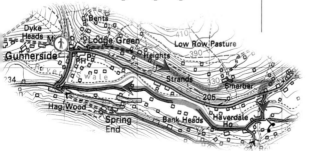

127

sharp bend of a gravel track. Continue down the hill for a further 200m to pass a small garage, where you should then leave the track, doubling back beside the bottom wall of the field past a barn. Approaching trees near the corner, bear left to find a developing track into the wood. Through a gate at the bottom, keep left again to emerge onto a lane.

Turn left and almost immediately right along the narrow lane across **Isles Bridge**, signed to Crackpot. Keep right at the next junction, and then at a fork below the Gables, bear off right along **Dubbing Garth**. Beyond Haverdale House the way degrades to a leafy track, which soon closes with the river. Eventually, however, the two part company, the track cutting a bend in the river and later climbing above a steep, wooded bank. It ultimately leads out to the main lane through Swaledale above **Gunnerside New Bridge**.

The 'old bridge' across the Swale, together with much of the road leading from it into the village, was washed away during **floods** that swept down the dale following a great storm in July 1888. The decision to build a replacement bridge was finally taken in June the following year, and the 'new bridge' completed in January 1890. But inundation is an ever-present risk along the narrow valley of this fast-flowing river, and only the following year the bridge was in the news again as yet another torrent threatened its existence. Happily, it survived this, and the many others that have since thundered through, justifying the £1000 that the Richmond Highways Board reluctantly expended upon it.

Cross the bridge and walk back into the village.

On the left is a **Wesleyan chapel** set within its own graveyard. The non-conformist denominations found an enthusiastic following amongst the hardworking Dales folk, not least because churches were few and far between. The chapel here was

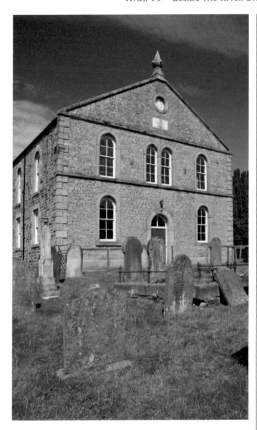

Gunnerside Methodist Church, rebuilt in 1866 for a growing congregation

founded in 1789, just two years before the death of John Wesley, one of the founders of the Methodist movement, who had visited the area as part of his preaching mission to the labouring classes. The early decades of the following century saw the lead industry boom, bringing an influx of men to work in the mines, together with their families. The resulting growth in the congregation necessitated the building of this larger chapel in 1866.

129

WALK 20

Gunnerside Gill

Start	Gunnerside (SD950982)
Distance	7 miles (11.3km)
Height gain	480m (1575ft)
Time	3hr
Terrain	Moorland tracks and paths
OS map	Explorer OL30 – Yorkshire Dales (Northern & Central Areas)
Refreshments	The King's Head and Ghyllfoot Tearoom in Gunnerside
Toilets	Beside the King's Head
Parking	In village centre near bridge

Gunnerside is superbly placed for any number of satisfying walks, but the most popular is undoubtedly this one, which follows a deep fold into the hills behind the village, past a long string of lead mines, hushes and dressing floors. Nature has softened the industrial dereliction, and many of the buildings have collapsed, but there remains more than enough to create a vivid impression of what this corner of the Dales must have been like 150 years ago.

Leave the village along a track almost opposite the King's Head, going upstream beside **Gunnerside Beck**. Just before the last building, a converted chapel, keep an eye open for a stepped path discreetly signed off on the right. It skirts the buildings and continues up the valley across a glade and into woodland.

After briefly flirting with the boulders beside the stream, it takes an elevated line as the valley narrows, losing sight of and, at one point, even the sound of the dashing water. Higher up, the path drops from the trees across a side-stream to find the valley floor opened out. Crossing a stile, continue by the wall, shortly passing the Sir Francis dressing floor.

*Gunnerside Little Bridge
beside the King's Head*

THE SIR FRANCIS MINE

The Sir Francis mine opened in 1864 and was named for the son of the land-owner, Sir George Denys. An ambitious venture to exploit seams deep within the hill, it was the first to employ compressed air drills. The compressor was powered by a water wheel and the air stored in a massive iron tank. The new drills were effective in shattering the hard rock, and had the additional advantage that the exhausts pumped air into the mine, saving the cost of a ventilation system, but the noise levels suffered by the miners in the constricted, echoing levels must have been horrendous.

Above the dressing floor is a row of stone bunkers, known as bouse teems. These were used to hold the ore produced by each gang of miners, for calculating individual payment, which was based on the amount of lead actually yielded and not what the miners dug out.

The material brought from the mine was crushed on the dressing floor and then sorted and washed to separate the galena – the lead-bearing ore – from the waste. The rubbish was just dumped in the barren heaps seen all around and only the ore carted away to the smelt furnace. The operation was remarkably efficient, and precious little useable ore was left in the tips, although the mine, never very profitable, was abandoned in the 1880s.

Carrying on over a stile, the path takes a higher route above rough grazing enclosures, later passing the Dolly

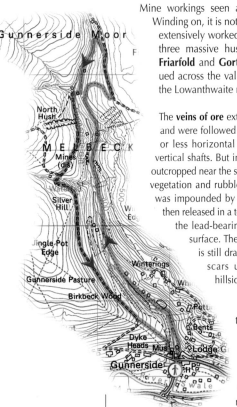

Mine workings seen above the opposite bank. Winding on, it is not then far to one of the most extensively worked areas in the valley, where three massive hushes converge – **Bunting**, **Friarfold** and **Gorton**. The rich veins continued across the valley and were worked from the Lowanthwaite mines and hushes.

The **veins of ore** extend deep underground, and were followed using a system of more or less horizontal tunnels, or drifts, and vertical shafts. But in some places the veins outcropped near the surface. To strip away the vegetation and rubble covering them, water was impounded by dams high above, and then released in a torrential flood to expose the lead-bearing ore just beneath the surface. The extent of these hushes is still dramatically evident in the scars upon the surrounding hillsides.

At a four-way junction, take the path ahead signed to the Blakethwaite Dams. The way wanders up through the workings, revealing a surprisingly wild beauty where the ravages of man have been tempered by nature.

As the path later begins to fall, branch right, rising across a steep slope of bare scree. Opposite, at the foot of Blind Gill is the Blakethwaite Smelt Mill, which you will get a closer look at on the return. Passing into heather, watch for the path swinging right and climbing to a broad moorland track.

Follow the track left for 500m, keeping your eyes open for a small pile of stones that marks the beginning of a hardly discernible path branching down into the valley. After an initial steep drop across a bank of heather, the way levels and becomes more obvious, continuing a little further up the valley before swinging back on itself in more earnest descent, and giving a superb view down the rugged dale. It eventually meets the river by more ruined buildings.

It is often possible to cross the stream here and follow the path on the opposite side down to **Blakethwaite Smelt Mill**. But after heavy rain it is best to remain on this bank, following a clear trail past a small waterfall and rising through the bracken. Coming level with Blind Gill, a cairn marks a narrower path that zigzags down to the mill. The main stream is now easily crossed on a sturdy bridge made from a single slab of stone, and Blind Gill has ample boulders and rocks to furnish a dry-shod passage, once you have explored the site and are ready to continue.

The arched wall of the peat store by the Botcher Gill smelt mill

BLAKETHWAITE SMELT MILL

Lead ore has been mined in Gunnerside since at least the 15th century, but output peaked at the beginning of the 1900s. The ore had formerly been carted away for smelting elsewhere, but the amount then being produced justified smelting on site, and a mill was built at the foot of Blind Gill to deal with the ore from the Blakethwaite and Lowanthwaite operations.

The furnace was sited below the cliff, between the two streams, and although the building is now mostly a ruin, the four cast-iron pillars that supported the furnace arches still stand proud above the rubble. The course of the flue is visible too, extending straight up the cliff behind, but the chimney at the top has collapsed. Partway up the scar, beside the flue, is a lime kiln, used for making mortar. The furnace was fuelled largely by peat, dug from the upper moors. It was brought down on sleds and stored in the big building on the eastern bank of the stream. The large arches provided ventilation to dry it off before it could be used. Coal was also burnt, carried down from the mines at Tan Hill.

A broad path starts back down the valley, rising gently along the steep slopes that drop to the stream. A bridge takes the route over North Hush, whose true extent was revealed from the opposite side, and the way continues above the Dolly mines to a junction overlooking **Botcher Gill**. The track to the right leads over the moors to Swinner Gill, near Keld, and from it a track branches north to the summit of Rogan's Seat, the easiest way up for those wanting to bag the summit.

The way back, however, follows the track across Botcher Gill, an easy and pleasant walk enhanced by the view down the valley into Swaledale. After 1¼ miles (2.4km) the track curves right around the nose of the hill. Leave it there, branching off onto a descending path that parts the rough grazing. The trod eventually falls to a fence, turning with it in search of a gate, which tips you out into Gunnerside, just above the parking area.

WALK 21
Ivelet Bridge from Muker

Start	Muker (SD910978)
Distance	5 miles (8km)
Height gain	250m (820ft)
Time	2hr
Terrain	Moorland and riverside trods
OS map	Explorer OL30 – Yorkshire Dales (Northern & Central Areas)
Refreshments	The Farmers Arms and the Village Store & Tea Shop in Muker
Toilets	At Muker
Parking	National park car park at edge of village (pay and display)

Much of the stunning beauty of the northern Dales is contained within its valleys, as demonstrated on this leisurely ramble from the picturesque village of Muker. Setting out along the rougher grazing pastures of the southern hillside, there are superb, far-reaching views along the dale, while the return follows the riverside meadows from an impressive pack-horse bridge. Keep your eyes open for moorland birds, such as curlew and lapwing, while down by the river you might spot oystercatchers and wagtails.

MUKER

Muker stands at the foot of Kisdon, overlooking the confluence of the two valleys that define the hill – Straw Beck, a prehistoric channel of the Swale, and the river's present course below its eastern flank. The sheltered riverside meadows attracted Norse settlers in the ninth century, who gave the place a name, Mjor-aker, meaning the 'narrow acre'.

Muker remained a remote settlement throughout the Middle Ages, and it was not until 1580 that the church was built. St Mary's is one of the few churches in England put up just after the English Reformation under Elizabeth I, and is the highest in the dale. Although marriage and burial rights were then conferred upon the village priest (thus ending the long trek down the valley to the mother church), the fees still went to Grinton's vicar, a bone of contention that remained for 170 years. St Mary's tower clock, installed to commemorate the coronation of George V and Mary in 1911, has, unusually, two faces, looking out to the south and the west.

The village significantly expanded with the development of the local lead mining industry in the 18th century, and the Victorian zeal for self-betterment resulted in a school, public hall, and an ornately fronted literary institute. The forerunners of our present-day public libraries, such institutions brought a wide range of books within reach of ordinary people, and encouraged reading for pleasure as well as study for improvement.

Leave the car park beside the bridge in **Muker** as if to follow the lane towards Gunnerside, but immediately bear off onto a bridleway signed as the 'Occupation Road'. Climb up the hillside for ¼ mile (400m) to a bend just beyond a couple of barns. Go through the second of the two gates on the left and follow an undulating path away beside the wall. The way eventually emerges onto a track beside a cottage at **Rash**. Accompany it down to a bridge, just beyond which, turn right and climb towards another cottage.

Reaching the entrance, pass through a gap stile on the right and bear left to another stile. Carry on up the hill beside the left boundary, eventually reaching a barn. From there, strike a diagonal to meet the upper wall at its high point. Cross and go through a field gate to the left and then bear right over the moor, leaving through a narrow gate onto a lane.

Follow it up the hill for ¼ mile (400m) to a gate on the left. Head out across the rough pasture, bypassing the left-hand corner of **Kearton's Wood** to find a squeeze stile in the far wall. Walk away, maintaining height above the deepening wooded gully of Oxnop Beck, before dropping towards **Low Oxnop Farm**, which soon comes into view. Skirt the buildings to the right and then slip through a squeeze stile into the adjacent field. Bear right above the stream, eventually descending to gain the lane beside **Oxnop Bridge**.

Just over the bridge, turn down a by-lane, which falls to the River Swale at graceful, high-arched **Ivelet Bridge**. On the northern bank, go through a gate on the left and follow a trod that meanders upstream through a succession of riverside meadows.

A mile (1.6km) of easy walking eventually brings you to a wall stile, where a signpost to **Ramps Holme Bridge** directs you away from the river. Carry on past Ramps Holme Farm, following the path for a further ¼ mile (400m) to reach a fork, there dropping left to a footbridge across the River Swale.

Take the path up the valley until you reach an isolated barn, doubling back around it onto a grass track that rises towards trees. Becoming enclosed, it gives a grand view across the valley, eventually leading to a gravel lane. That in turn takes you back into the village, where refreshments are served in both the village pub and teashop.

The River Swale above Ramps Holme Bridge

WALK 22

Great Shunner Fell and
Lovely Seat from Thwaite

Start	Thwaite (SD892980)
Distance	9½ miles (15.3km)
Height gain	780m (2559ft)
Time	4hr30
Terrain	Moorland paths and trods; return along a lane
OS map	Explorer OL30 – Yorkshire Dales (Northern & Central Areas)
Refreshments	Kearton Country Hotel and Tearooms in Thwaite
Toilets	None
Parking	Small lay-by near the junction with the Buttertubs road south of Thwaite
Note	Dogs are not allowed on Open Access land away from rights of way

Great Shunner Fell lies on the Pennine Way between Hardraw and Thwaite, and is therefore blessed with good paths from either side to ease the passage of the many who tramp by on their pilgrimage. Its neighbour, Lovely Seat – pronounced 'Lunnerset' – is completely bypassed, and therefore not so fortunate, but can be easily attained from the road at the top of the pass separating the two. This route takes in both tops and returns along the lane, giving ample opportunity to peer into the abyss of the Buttertubs.

Walk through the village in the direction of Keld. As the lane rises away, leave through a gate on the left, from which a path is signed across the meadows above Thwaite Beck to Great Shunner Fell. Encountering rougher pasture in the third field, head up from the stream to find a gated stile in the top wall and continue across a narrow enclosure to emerge onto a track.

To the left, the track climbs easily away, a superb view opening behind along the valley into Swaledale.

Thwaite

Ahead rise Great and Little Shunner fells, a mass of high moorland enclosing the head of Thwaite Beck, while over to the left is Muker Common, culminating in Lovely Seat. The track continues a little way above the intake, finally giving out as it approaches low heaps of bare shale.

> Although Swaledale is noted more for its lead mines, the layers of the Yoredale Series also contain thin seams of **coal**. Small mines such as this provided fuel for cottage hearths, as well as field lime kilns and smelting, but most closed in the 1880s in the face of competition from the railway, which brought in cheaper and better coal.

The onward path, for the most part, is now paved all the way to the summit of **Great Shunner Fell**, rising steadily in a great sweep along the peaty northern ridge of the hill.

> Wide views open across Birkdale to Nine Standards Rigg, while further south is High Seat and Hugh Seat. The conspicuous body of water to

be seen on the moor across the valley is **Birkdale Tarn**. Although the third largest lake in the Dales, it is not entirely natural, being extended from an originally much smaller tarn to provide a reliable water supply for the area's lead mines.

A steepening gradient takes the path to a prominent drystone pillar, and then, after a short level stretch, a final pull brings the summit shelter wall suddenly into view.

The quick way back is simply to retrace your steps, enjoying a fantastic panorama all the way. More challenging is to strike out across Little Shunner Fell to the lane at the top of the Buttertubs Pass. Less daunting than it may seem, the route follows the fence line all the way down, while the ground underfoot, although often wet, is not as boggy as might be expected.

Head southeast from the shelter, following the fence to a stile. Continue on its northern flank, the ground dropping more steeply to a broad terrace. Meeting the end of a stone wall, the way now swings left towards the plateau of **Little Shunner Fell**, avoiding the deepening fold of Fossdale Gill. At Little Shunner, curve right past its 'summit', marked by a pathetic pile of stones on the opposite side of the fence, setting a course on Lovely Seat, which rises across the head of the pass.

The trod occasionally leaves the fence in search of the firmest passage through the low peat hags, but never moves far away. After crossing the bleakly named Grimy Gutter Hags, the fence abruptly swings right, seemingly taking you completely off course. However, to ignore it would land you with an uncomfortably steep descent, so accept its guidance and stick with it to the road.

Lovely Seat rises straight in front of you, a mere 150m of climbing. Simply follow the fence up the hill for ¾ mile (1.2km) to the top, where there is indeed a lovely seat from which to enjoy the view, dominated to the south by the Yorkshire Three Peaks gathered around the head of Ribblesdale. Return to the road and follow it north down the hill past the spectacular Buttertubs.

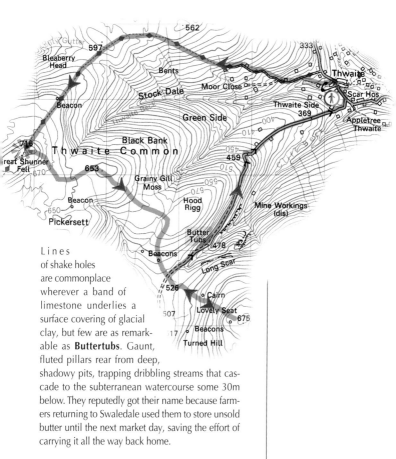

Lines of shake holes are commonplace wherever a band of limestone underlies a surface covering of glacial clay, but few are as remarkable as **Buttertubs**. Gaunt, fluted pillars rear from deep, shadowy pits, trapping dribbling streams that cascade to the subterranean watercourse some 30m below. They reputedly got their name because farmers returning to Swaledale used them to store unsold butter until the next market day, saving the effort of carrying it all the way back home.

After a brief pull, the road drops along the steep valley side above Cliff Beck, a deep cleft continuing the dramatic theme set by the Buttertubs. Piles of rubble from extensive lead workings litter the opposite slopes, and the dark openings of adits hint again of an unseen world below ground.

Further down, the gradient runs out between the hay meadows of the lower valley, dotted with laithes that were used to store hay and over-winter the stock. The long but pleasant walk finally returns you to the junction by the lay-by at the edge of Thwaite.

WALK 23

*Muker, Thwaite and Kisdon Force
from Keld*

Start	Keld (NY892012)
Distance	8¼ miles (13.3km)
Height gain	485m (1591ft)
Time	3hr30
Terrain	Field trods and tracks
OS map	Explorer OL30 – Yorkshire Dales (Northern & Central Areas)
Refreshments	Snacks at Park Lodge Farm, tearoom/coffee shop and pub at both Muker and Thwaite
Toilets	At both Keld and Muker
Parking	Park Lodge Farm at Keld (honesty box)

Before the last glaciation, the River Swale flowed in the valley cutting the western side of Kisdon Hill. But retreating ice blocked it with a moraine, and the pent-up water forced a passage around the eastern flank, completely separating the hill from the surrounding high ground, and creating its unusual topography. While you can simply climb to its top from Muker, this enjoyable walk links the three villages at its foot, and explores the superb scenery of the gorge and Kisdon Side, a designated SSSI.

Head back out of the car park and keep ahead across the end of the turning area to a walled track marked as the Coast to Coast trail. Soon reaching a fork, bear left with the Pennine Way, dropping to a bridge across the River Swale. The path winds left and right, climbing to a junction beside the foaming cascades of **East Gill**.

Turn across the bridge and follow the track, rising above a deepening sylvan gorge that hides impressive Kisdon Force, which can be visited on the return. For the present, content yourself with the striking view along the valley, and scuffing the gravel of the path in search of fossil fragments.

These fossils, looking like petrified, wrinkled ciga-
rette filters, are the remains of pieces of **crinoid**, a
strange plant-like animal that inhabited the warm
prehistoric seas. Sometimes known as sea lilies,
they first appeared over 480 million years ago,
and, showing a remarkable adaptivity in survival,
still exist today.

Wind below the foot of the Beldi Hill lead mines,
ignoring a path off on the left, which rises above Crackpot
Hall and more abandoned workings and across the moor
to the head of Gunnerside Gill.

There is a good view across to ruined **Crackpot
Hall** on the way back. The site of a hunting lodge
that may originally date to the beginning of the 16th
century, when red deer roamed
the valley, the present building was constructed around
1750, and has variously
served as a lodge, farm-
house and mine offices.
Mining subsidence in
the 1950s brought its
final demise, but
recent stabilisa-
tion will ensure it
remains a stark
landmark on
the hillside. Its
curious name
derives not
from the men-
tal state of its
erstwhile inhab-
itants, but from
the Old Norse lan-
guage, and refers to a
cave used by crows as
a roost.

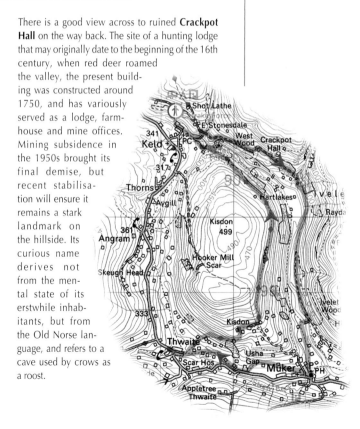

Breaking from the cliffs and gorges that confined its course higher up, the river finds freedom in the flat bottom of a wider flood plain.

Continue along the main valley, the path now beginning to lose height and twisting to the foot of **Swinner Gill**, where the ruin of a smelt mill is another reminder of the levels that burrowed into the hill following the rich seams of lead ore. Cross the stream and climb away, quickly leaving behind the ruggedness of the upper valley. ◄

The houses and squat-towered church of Muker eventually come into view, and shortly, **Ramps Holme Bridge**, across the Swale. Where the path then divides, stay low, delving into trees to reach a second branch, signed to Muker, which drops to the bridge.

On the opposite bank, head briefly back upstream and over a stile, to find a stepped stile in the accompanying wall a little further on. From this, a path leads across a succession of delightful hay meadows to the village. Keep ahead through the back streets to emerge onto the main lane, where you will find the toilets (opposite) and the pub and teashop just to the right.

That the lead mines brought people and prosperity to the village is reflected in its **institutions**. The church was restored, a chapel built, and also a public hall and literary institute erected, all of which still stand, although not necessarily used for their original purpose. The church, dedicated to St Mary the Virgin, was one of the few to be built during the reign of the first Queen Elizabeth, a chapel of ease to the mother church down the valley at Grinton.

As an alternative to simply following the lane on to Thwaite, you can, instead, take the old Corpse Road, a delightful path across the meadows. In early summer they are awash with the subtle colour of buttercups, cranesbill, daisies, pignut and clover, and one of the great enchantments of this corner of the Dales.

From the main lane, retrace your steps into the village. Swing left in front of the entrance to the church, along a path opposite the public hall that narrows between cottages. Emerging onto a track, continue past another row of cottages to a gate at the end, from which an intermittently flagged path heads away across a succession of fields.

> The **Corpse Road** was once used to bring the dead from the upper valley for burial at the parish church in Grinton, a long and arduous journey, particularly in the depths of winter. But surely the coffin bearers could not have been faced with the innumerable narrow stiles encountered by today's walkers – imagine the conversation in passing through with such a heavy and cumbersome load: 'T' thee', 'Yon end up a bit', 'Nay, not that a way', 'Careful' – 'Oh 'eck'.

The path eventually leads to **Usha Gap Farm**. Walk through the yard to the lane and turn right to a bridge. As the lane swings to cross it, go ahead through a gate and follow a path signed to Thwaite. Emerging into a small field, continue by the right fence. Slip through a gate and walk past the end of a barn to a gated stile in the end wall. Carry on to another stile in the corner, through which cross the delicate skeleton arch of an ancient stone bridge.

RICHARD AND CHERRY KEARTON

The name of the pub and coffee shop at Thwaite celebrates the village's illustrious sons, Richard and Cherry Kearton. Born in 1862 and 1871 respectively to a farming family, an affinity for the outdoors followed as a matter of course, but after a childhood accident that left Richard partly crippled, he developed a keen interest in the natural world. His ability to call the grouse on the shoot brought him to the notice of Sidney Galpin, whose father was one of the founders of the Cassell publishing house. Richard was subsequently offered a job there, and exploited his love of wildlife as a writer, lecturer and broadcaster. He later joined forces with his brother, who pioneered wildlife photography, and their first collaboration, British Birds' Nests and Egg Collecting, published in 1895, defined a new era in publishing. Cherry went on to develop many innovative techniques, such as camouflaged cameras and aerial photography, and between them they did much to popularise natural history.

Climbing from Thwaite onto the flanks of Kisdon Hill

Over the bridge, turn right and continue across more fields towards the cottages of **Thwaite**. At a stile just before a farm, the ongoing path is signed off to the right, the Pennine Way to Keld. But first it is worth continuing ahead beside the farm for a quick look around the attractive hamlet, a pleasing collection of cottages gathered around the Kearton Country Hotel and coffee shop.

Return past the farm to the junction and follow the Pennine Way left across a couple of meadows towards Keld. Over a stream, swing right into the field corner, and then climb at its edge to a squeeze gate at the top. The path then slants to the right, rising across a steep hillside of bilberry, heather and bracken, from which a splendid prospect opens ahead along the valley past Muker into Swaledale.

Higher up, an abrupt change in vegetation signifies the transition to limestone. Gone is the heath, replaced by short-cropped grass that conceals a host of tiny flowers. Levelling off, the path winds through old enclosures to a hilltop farm, **Kisdon**.

Pass behind the farmhouse to emerge at the end of a track, but instead of following it, take the gate on the left. A contained grass track rises past a lime kiln to end by a small barn. Keeping with the Pennine Way, bear right at the junction there, dropping to a second junction by another barn.

Go left, the path briefly climbing before running easily through a succession of hillside enclosures, from which there is a superb view along the valley. Swimmer Gill enters on the bend of the river, its course surrounded by the extensive heaps of rubble and ruined buildings of old mining enterprise.

> In 1769, the Parkes Company discovered a valuable seam of ore, and the valley became a **battleground** for an embittered dispute over land ownership. This part of the valley had been the property of the Whartons, but the family was disgraced, and forfeited most of their lands after Philip, the first duke, lost his fortune in the collapse of the South Sea Bubble, and then committed treason by siding with the Jacobite cause. Lord Pomfret believed the land on which the strike was made came to him via his wife, a descendant of Wharton. His unsuccessful claim ruined him, and sparked a rash of sabotage between the opposing mines.

Rounding the corner into the upper part of the valley, the path starts to lose height above rich woodland of ash, birch and hazel, a remnant of the wild wood that once filled the dale. Towards the far end of the trees, the Pennine Way is signed through a gap in the wall down to Keld.

Below, the Swale is squeezed through a narrowing gorge, confined by the almost blue cliffs on the far side. Here, hidden from view, is Keld's most dramatic waterfall, Kisdon Force. Carry on, before long joined by another path from the right, and continue to a second path, which is signed back to **Kisdon Force**. Worth the detour, the way drops below the cliffs of this side of the valley, where a pillar stands precariously detached from the rock face. The path descends to a shelf above the falls, although the last bit is something of a scramble, as the path has slipped away and can be slippery when wet.

Retrace your steps to the Pennine Way and continue towards **Keld**. The way, shortly becoming contained, meets the outward route and returns you to the village.

WALK 24

*Whitsundale and the
head of the River Swale*

Start	Keld (NY892012)
Distance	8 miles (12.9km)
Height gain	365m (1197ft)
Time	3hr15
Terrain	Tracks and moorland trods
OS map	Explorer OL30 – Yorkshire Dales (Northern & Central Areas)
Refreshments	Snacks at Park Lodge Farm and Ravenseat Farm
Toilets	At both car park and in village
Parking	Park Lodge Farm, Keld (honesty box)

The River Swale is said to be the fastest-flowing river in England, and it is therefore not surprising that its upper reaches are well blessed with waterfalls. While none are particularly high, they can all be impressive after rain, and add another dimension to this quietly superb walk, which peaks into one of the lesser-known dales before passing the source of the River Swale.

Head back out of the car park and cross the end of the turning circle to a walled track opposite, a bridleway signed 'Coast to Coast'. Where that then forks, drop left, joining the Pennine Way to a bridge across the River Swale. Swinging left and then forking right, the path climbs to a junction beside **East Gill**, as it tumbles over three rocky steps to join the River Swale.

KELD

Keld is the highest village in the dale, and was first settled by Norse sheep farmers, who gave it its name, meaning 'stream'. Here, near the Swale's source and surrounded by high moorland hills, the valley is perhaps at its most beautiful. Flowing along a rugged streambed and nourished by innumerable side-becks, the river splashes over limestone steps and through a succession of cramped gorges. Where the valley floor widens, the river is bordered by ribbons of hay meadow, which are amongst the most glorious you will find anywhere in the country. Early summer is their best time, when they burst into delicate colour, pastel shades of yellow, purple and white, which resolve into countless buttercups, daisies, clover heads, and cranesbill. The delicate, branched white flower heads are pignut, a member of the carrot family, so named because pigs were once trained to grub out the roots, which were then collected as food. Here, though, once the flowers have seeded, the fields are cut for hay, which is stored for winter fodder.

Turn left with the Pennine Way as far as **East Stonesdale Farm**, but in the yard, bear off left through a gate along a bridleway. The broad track gently undulates across the hillside, giving an excellent prospect over the hay meadows of the upper part of the dale. ▸ Further along, the path winds to cross a bridge over **Stonesdale Beck**, where there is yet another cascade, Currack Force.

However, leave the track just before the bridge, through a gate on the right, and head into the side-valley of West Stones Dale. Briefly follow the stream before being forced onto higher ground above a wooded cleft. Shortly after passing through a gate, look in the trees for a foot-bridge spanning the ghyll. Briefly double back

Glimpsed below, the river runs behind the village at the foot of limestone cliffs concealing a couple of waterfalls, Catrake Force and Hoggarts Leap.

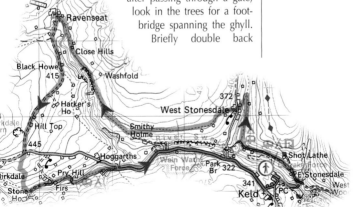

along the opposite bank until you reach a wall, and then climb away beside it to **West Stonesdale Farm**, leaving through a gate in the corner and past the farmhouse to emerge onto a lane.

Go left to a telephone box, then turn off right, passing through a gate to follow a wall above the deep gully of a stream. Leave the gully where the wall then kinks left, sticking at the edge of the rough upland grazing.

As the wall later loses height, the right of way remains high, contouring the shoulder of the hill into Whitsundale. But, with no evident path on the ground, it is easier to remain by the wall, continuing beyond its eventual corner to join a well-trodden path emerging from a gate at the bottom.

Part of the northern Coast to Coast long-distance path, the way toddles on into the delightful fold of **Whitsundale**. Below, the beck foams over endless stony steps, while at Oven Mouth and How Edge, it twists dramatically to find weaknesses in bands of harder rock.

Yellow spots confirm the course of the path through a succession of pastures, eventually closing with the stream above a small fall and leading to the remote settlement of **Ravenseat**. Follow the track left across a flat bridge and past the entrance to Ravenseat Farm, where you can buy tea and scones. Continue over a charming pack-horse bridge across Whitsundale Beck and head away along the narrow lane.

The tarmac makes for easy walking, and detracts nothing from the pleasure of the view into Swaledale as it curves around the slope of the hill. Meeting the main lane at the bottom, go right, but then after 50m, bear off left onto a descending track that winds down to the river at the foot of **Birkdale**. It is here that Birkdale Beck and Great Sleddale Beck come together as the River Swale.

At a junction of paths by a very substantial 19th-century bridge near Stone House, go left beside a pretty stretch of river bordered by hay meadows. Becoming contained, the path soon leads to a farm. Walk beyond the farmhouse across a yard to a field gate, and bear left through a second gate to pass a barn on your right. Through a gap beside it, carry on across a field, rejoining the river down to another bridge identical to that at Stone House.

On the far bank the path continues downstream, but is then pushed away beside a wall to a barn at the foot of a narrow gully, Great Ash Gill. Through a gate, go left beside the stream, joining a track at the end of the wall. Cross the stream and walk out to meet the lane by **Hoggarths Bridge**.

Follow the lane down the valley, shortly passing below the sheer limestone cliffs of Cotterby Scar. Towards the far end of the escarpment, the river surges over **Wain Wath Force**, where there is a small picnic area. Beyond the turning to Tan Hill, the lane takes a higher course above the meadows for the last half mile (800m). Go left at the next junction to return to the village, passing the small but interesting heritage centre by the church.

Wain Wath Force on the River Swale

**PART 4
WENSLEYDALE AND
COVERDALE**

At Aysgill Force, the beck tumbles over a cliff of tufa (Walk 34)

WALK 25

A walk in Coverdale

Start	Carlton (SE069847)
Distance	6½ miles (10.5km)
Height gain	260m (853ft)
Time	2hr30
Terrain	Field trods
OS map	Explorer OL30 – Yorkshire Dales (Northern & Central Areas)
Refreshments	Pubs at Carlton and Horsehouse
Toilets	None
Parking	Car park by village hall at eastern end of Carlton (honesty box)

Despite its obvious beauty and the fact that a road runs right through, Coverdale is one of the lesser-known dales. This walk wanders through the fields of its middle reaches, linking two of the small but endearingly attractive villages speckled along its length. A couple of pubs and a delightful stretch by the river add to the enjoyment, and will undoubtedly inspire further exploration of this unspoiled corner.

From the car park walk into the village, leaving the lane beside a barn just before the **Forester's Arms**, at a signpost to Goodman's Gill. However, rather than follow the track, bear left to a stile and continue along the top of a grass bank above the stream. The path shortly falls to a footbridge, but instead, go left to a small gate, passing into a field beside a barn.

Strike out to a stile near the far right corner, maintaining the same line in the next field to come out onto a narrow, walled track. Go right and, at the bottom, right again, slanting across the head of a field to a gate at the far side. Back above Goodman's Gill, follow a descending path that leads to a footbridge, shaded by the trees above its confluence with the **River Cover**. A second bridge takes you over the main river.

COVERHAM ABBEY

The monks of Coverham Abbey were indeed richly blessed when they were endowed with lands in this beautiful dale. Premonstratensian Canons, they arrived from Swainby Abbey near Leeming on the banks of the River Swale, relocated, it is said, so that their benefactor, Ranulphus Fitz-Robert, would be able to hear the abbey bells from his castle at Middleham. Although only a small house, it held lands and churches not only in Coverdale, but as far away as Sedbergh, and Seaham in County Durham, and, despite a period of great poverty, survived until the Dissolution, when the abbey passed into secular hands. It was sited beside the river some 3 miles (4.8km) to the northwest, but only a few relics remain of the original buildings.

Climb away at the field edge to a small gate. The line of the path then swings right to a signpost, before continuing straight up the hill once more to a kissing-gate in the top wall. However, instead of passing through towards West Scrafton (which in the past made at least part of its living from coal mining high on the hills above), go right to a fence stile in the side boundary. Carry on to a stile in the far right corner and then walk left to a stile. Keep going to the distant corner of the next meadow, where a couple of gates take you out onto a narrow lane. Amble down to a bridge spanning the River Cover.

Just before the bridge, take a gravel track signed off to Swineside. After some 150m, look for an angled path up the wooded bank to a field at the top. Continue climbing on a right diagonal, making for a redundant stile in the upper corner. Walk on to a fence stile and then strike out to a squeeze stile situated in the end of a short length of wall.

Keep going across another field and on below a wall. Approaching the corner, slip through a gate and bear right to a fence stile. An intermediate signpost guides you on a slanting path up the hillside to a ladder stile by an indented wall corner. Carry on along the bottom boundary to emerge behind a cluster of converted barns at **Swineside**. Pass ahead through the gardens to come out at the end of a farm lane.

The remote hamlet of Swineside

Bear right past cottages to a gate by a barn standing at the end of the track. The way, signed to Horsehouse, continues straight ahead across the hillside through a succession of rough pastures across Rampshaw Bank.

The view opens to reveal the upper reaches of the valley, bound on the left by a long ridge of bare hills. Great Haw and Dead Man's Hill run on to Little Whernside, while in the far distance the ground rises to the highest point, Great Whernside. Set back on the opposite side of the valley are the Height of Hazely and Hartland Hill, with Brown Haw narrowing the head of the valley as it rises to a high pass over which the road climbs to reach Kettlewell in Wharfedale.

After some 650m, cross a trickling spring to a gap stile. A sign indicates

155

Through the meadows to Horsehead

the onward path, now inclining across the hillside to a stile beside a gate in the bottom wall. Through that, bear left, crossing Woods Gill to another stile. Angle on across the slope, fording a stream to encounter yet one more stile.

Pass through the corner of a woodland plantation, leaving beside an unusual tree, where ash and hawthorn have almost fused into a single entity. Keep going towards **Hindlethwaite Hall Farm**, making for a stile just to the right of two gates. Cross a small paddock and then a track to find a footbridge spanning the River Cover.

To reach **Horsehouse**, go left to a gate and bear right across the next field. Through a gate at the far side, continue the line to another gate in the top wall and head up along a narrow enclosure to come out on a back lane in front of a row of cottages. The main lane and village centre is just to the left.

Return to the footbridge, but now remain on this bank. Walk downstream, later crossing a farm track by a bridge. Ignoring a subsequent sign to Gammersgill, continue beside the river for a further ½ mile (800m). Eventually reaching a gated squeeze stile beneath a

HORSEHOUSE

Despite its size, the charming village of Horsehouse has the two institutions where life's great milestones are traditionally celebrated, a church and a pub, facing each other across the narrow lane in the heart of the village.

Dedications to St Botolph are not common in the north, his name today associated more with East Anglia and around the Thames, where he founded a monastery and several churches. As with many of the early saints, his history is clouded, but nevertheless Botolph is regarded as one of the great preaching missionaries of the seventh century. There is confusion as to whether he was a Scot, a Saxon or even Irish, but he studied in Germany and, on his return, was granted by the king land at Ikenhoe to build a monastery. Contenders for its location are Boston in Lincolnshire and Iken in Suffolk, but wherever, it is known that Botolph was visited there, before his death in AD680, by the Northumbrian abbot St Ceolfrid, who held him in high esteem. His monastic community continued in the Benedictine way of life for almost 200 years, before it was sacked in AD870 and its true location lost.

The tiny church here was rebuilt in the 19th century, and retains the simple candleholders that provided illumination before electricity came to the village. Like the church, the Thwaite Arms too is tiny, but not always open midweek lunchtime during the winter months.

The lane once formed part of the main highway between London and Richmond, and for centuries was travelled by trains of pack-horses, which rested in the village, hence its name. In later days, the stage mail also passed along the valley, crossing to Kettlewell in neighbouring Wharfedale over a high gap in the shadow of Great Whernside, where the gruelling incline of Park Rash must have been equally fearful in both ascent and descent.

telegraph pole, bear away from the river across a couple of pastures towards **Hall Farm**. Leave the fields to the right of the farmhouse, passing through an old paddock to emerge onto the lane in the hamlet of **Gammersgill**.

Turn right, crossing a bridge over the stream to find a path off signed to Carlton, some 200m along on the right. Cut a diagonal line across the meadow to come out onto the corner of an old, narrow green track, **Turnbeck Lane**. Ahead, it leads pleasantly on between the fields to a footbridge spanning Turn Beck.

Strike slightly right in the field beyond to a stile on the indented far corner of a wall, the way then fairly obviously continuing in a more or less straight line. It shortly leads past some very distinct old ploughing terraces, dips across the gully of a stream, and ultimately meets a narrow lane.

Follow the lane up the hill to a bend, where the continuing path to Carlton is again signed off. A trodden line starts you off, running on in the second meadow to a stile in the far left corner. Carry on beside the boundary wall and maintain the same line across more fields until, leaving through a gate, the path drops left into the wooded gully of **Goodman's Gill**. Cross the stream and follow your outward steps back into the village.

WALK 26

*West Witton and the
River Ure to Redmire Force*

Start	West Witton (SE067884)
Distance	5½ miles (8.9km)
Height gain	140m (459ft)
Time	2hr
Terrain	Tracks and field paths
OS map	Explorer OL30 – Yorkshire Dales (Northern & Central Areas)
Refreshments	Pubs and tea room in West Witton
Toilets	None
Parking	Lay-by beside A684, ¼ mile (400m) east of West Witton

Redmire Force, the lowest falls of the River Ure, also marks the point at which the river leaves the national park, although the boundary continues to follow the southern bank of the river further to the east. Less often visited than many other sections, it is a beautiful stretch of the river, and reached on this walk by attractive ancient lanes from the linear village of West Witton, nestling below the slopes of Penhill. Parking in the village itself is difficult, but there is a convenient lay-by beside the main road at its eastern boundary.

Entering the village from the east, look for a track, **Flatts Lane**, dropping right, just past the bus stop. After only a short distance, turn right again, into **Back Lane**, which weaves a convoluting course for some ¾ mile (1.2km) between flower-rich margins before ending at a squeeze stile.

Walking into a widening field, stick with the left-hand wall, maintaining your direction beyond its corner atop a grassy bank. The way shortly falls to meet a lower trod along which you should double back left across the bottom part of the pasture.

With wooded banks and rolling meadows, this is a particularly lovely section of the river, where you might spot oystercatchers, Canada geese, herons and the ubiquitous duck.

Passing through a gate in the end wall, cross a stream and then swing right at a three-way sign pointing to Hestholme Bridge. The path runs down above the stream to a stile and then curves to follow the bank of the River Ure upstream. ◄

Wanlass Park lay within the extensive **hunting forest** of Wensleydale, which was granted to the Lords of Richmond and Middleham. The 60 or so acres (24.3 hectares) overlooking the river were enclosed as a deer park, where the beasts were bred and allowed to roam free purely to provide sport for the lord and his favourites.

Low hillocks of glacial limestone deposit rumple the traditionally managed meadows, which contain many uncommon plants, including the winged and rare burnt orchids.

Upstream the flow of the Ure is divided around a wooded island, and above that, is broken over a wide, rocky bed. The path then climbs a high bank, the river running deep and narrow out of a sharp bend. Bearing right, the path drops from the bank to cut the curve across a flat expanse of meadow, and then joins a wall above another wooded bank overlooking a lazy backwater cut off from the main flow. ◄

Walking in the grazing pastures beside the River Ure

Coming to a ladder stile, cross and continue by the wall, soon reaching a narrow stile into the wood. The sound of cascading water heralds the proximity of Redmire Force, just ahead, the path winding down to the riverbank beside it.

> As if determined not to disappoint in its final rocky fling before the long journey down to the sea, the Ure creates an impressive scene as it cascades over the wide rocky cataracts of **Redmire Force.** Its relative inaccessibility means you can enjoy the spectacle without the company of the large crowds that sometimes throng the falls at Aysgarth, and the banks make a great spot for a quiet picnic.

You can, if you have the time, continue with the path above the river, upstream to the stepping-stones at Slapestone Wath, there linking with the ramble around Aysgarth Falls, described in Walk 28. To return to West Witton, go back through the wood and along the edge of the meadow to the ladder stile. However, instead of crossing, walk right on a field track, which, after passing along a second pasture meets a concrete track, part of **Back Lane**. Go left to its end and then bear right beside New Wood.

Carry on beyond the end of the wall, crossing the open field to join the opposite wall. Follow it over the crest of the low hill to a small gate tucked in the corner and keep with the ongoing wall to another gate near the far end.

The way continues for the next ½ mile (800m) as a pleasant, bounded old track that winds on between the fields. After bending on the approach to the main road, keep an eye open for a gate stile on the left, from which a path is signed to Witton.

Bear right to a gap stile, rising beyond onto a bank. Keep ahead to a gate at the end, from which a contained path winds out to the main road. Turn left through the village, passing its two pubs.

WITTON FEAST

On the Saturday closest to the feast day of St Bartholomew (24 August) is Witton Feast, a day of fun and frolicking that culminates in the 'Burning of Owd Bartle'. Bartle is a contraction of Bartholomew, but in the tradition here, which is said to go back 400 years, the effigy is certainly no saint. In one legend, he was a rustler, caught in the act high on Penhill and chased down towards the village, where he came to an untimely end. As the centrepiece of the fair, Owd Bartle is paraded through the village to the accompaniment of much high spirits, and an old rhyme that marks the course of his tragedy before finally being burnt.

> *In Penhill Crags he tore his rags;*
> *At Hunter's Thorn he blew his horn;*
> *At Capplebank Stee he brake his knee;*
> *At Grisgill Beck he brake his neck;*
> *At Wadham's End he couldn't fend;*
> *At Grisgill End he made his end.*
> *Shout, lads, shout.*

WALK 27

Aysgarth to West Burton

Start	Aysgarth Falls, Church Bank car park, Aysgarth (SE011884)
Distance	4½ miles (7.2km)
Height gain	175m (574ft)
Time	1hr45
Terrain	Tracks and field paths
OS map	Explorer OL30 – Yorkshire Dales (Northern & Central Areas)
Refreshments	Mill Race Teashop at Yore Mill, Fox and Hounds at West Burton
Toilets	At nearby national park visitor centre
Parking	Aysgarth Falls Church Bank car park (pay and display)

Aysgarth's falls are well known, but not quite so famous are those at nearby West Burton, an attractive village set around a sprawling green, and with an unusual, if not so ancient, village cross. The meandering route takes you through several clumps of woodland, each boasting a fine show of flowers in spring, and gives an albeit brief glimpse of the River Ure along the final leg. To spend more time by the river and view Aysgarth's main falls, the route can be linked with that described in Walk 28.

Begin by heading down the hill from the car park and turn in at the entrance to **St Andrew's Church**. Walk to the southern front of the church and go right, heading back through the churchyard and along a track to the main road.

Cross to a stile opposite, from which a path is signed to Eshington Bridge. Something of a switchback, it plunges first into a dip and then over a rise, before undulating more gently across a succession of fields, occasional signs confirming the route towards West Burton, soon visible ahead.

163

ST ANDREW'S CHURCH, AYSGARTH

St Andrew's is said to have the largest church graveyard in the country, and it extends over four acres (1.6 hectare). A 1000-year-old carved cross, found embedded in a nearby wall, but sadly later stolen, suggests that there has been a church here since at least the 10th century. Records table a list of vicars and rectors back to 1268, including one Alexander de Nevyel, who was consecrated Bishop of York in 1374.

Perhaps the most imposing features within the church are the vicar's stall and the rood screen, which originally stood in Jervaulx Abbey. Fashioned in 1472 and around 1506 respectively, they were brought here when the monks were evicted from the monastery at the Dissolution. The screen was subsequently moved to its present position in the choir after an extensive restoration of the church in 1866.

Emerging onto a lane, cross **Eshington Bridge**, but leave a few metres further on over a stile on the right. Head out across a couple of meadows to meet a bend of the stream and swing left over consecutive stiles. Continue along more fields past a barn, climbing out at the far side onto a lane. Almost opposite, a stepped path cuts through to a back lane in **West Burton** village. A short distance to the right, you will find the Fox and Hounds overlooking the expansive village green.

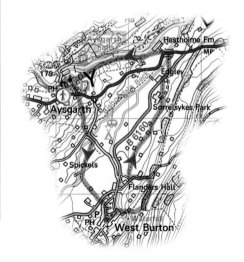

WEST BURTON

The green once hosted a medieval market, but the elaborate and striking octagonal pyramid cross dates only from 1820, and bears a resemblance to the monuments in Sorrelsykes Park, encountered later on. Unusually for a village, West Burton has no separate church, and lies within the Aysgarth parish, but in 1898 the Methodists built their own chapel.

West Burton Force is tucked out of obvious sight at the head of a small ravine, where Walden Beck tumbles over a low cliff of limestone. The pool into which the water cascades was originally dammed to provide power for a corn mill, but like several others in the area, the mill was installed with a turbine during the early years of the 20th century, bringing the first electricity to the village. The generator operated until 1948, when West Burton was finally connected to the National Grid, after which the mill was abandoned until it was more recently converted into holiday flats.

Walk down the green to the bottom corner, leaving along a track off right past the old mill house towards the waterfall. Cross the bridge below the falls to a stepped path zigzagging up through the trees on the far bank.

Follow a contained path away at the edge of a field, continuing beyond its end across another field to the corner of **Barrack Wood**. Mounting a stile, go left along the edge of the trees towards Morpeth Lane. ▶ Emerging into more open ground, the path drops out onto **Morpeth Gate**.

Go left, walking down past a farm and around a left bend. At a gate on the right, a path is then signed back across the fields to Edgley. Beyond the third field, carry on past a barn, making for a gate in the far corner. Keep going past another barn to emerge onto the edge of a large field. Bear left along its tree-lined boundary, passing through a stile into the next field. Walk on to cross a stream and then slant down a bank to meet a track behind **Sorrelsykes Farm**. Cross the track and keep ahead below a bank adorned with three impressive follies – a pepperpot, an arch and a spire. Reaching a waypost, bear left across the field to reach a lane opposite the house at **Edgley**.

Go right for 100m, and then, immediately after a track into the farm, pass through a gate on the left. Strike

Spring is one of the best times to pass by, when the undergrowth bursts into colour, with bluebells, clumps of ramsons, primroses and the humble buttercup, while here and there are patches of violet and orchids.

*Ransoms carpet
Hestholme Wood*

a diagonal across the field towards the middle of a wood to find a stile. A path winds down through the trees, in whose tops nest a noisy colony of rooks, to emerge onto the main road beside **Hestholme Bridge**.

If combining this walk with that to Aysgarth Falls (Walk 28), turn right. Otherwise, to return to the car park, go over the bridge and cross to the entrance of **Hestholme Farm** just around the bend. On the left of the drive, a footpath is signed through a small gate, heading diagonally out across the meadow.

Following the top of a wooded bank above the River Ure, continue at the edge of subsequent fields. The path briefly comes close to the water beside a small but none-theless impressive cataract, before climbing high above Aysgarth's **Lower Force**, of which there are only glimpses through the trees.

At the top of the rise, continue beside a fence to a stile into a small wood. Breaking out of the trees, carry on to St Andrew's churchyard and walk straight through to return to the lane just below the car park.

WALK 28

Aysgarth Falls

Start	Aysgarth Falls, Church Bank car park, Aysgarth (SE011884)
Distance	4 miles (6.4km)
Height gain	130m (426ft)
Time	1hr30
Terrain	Tracks and field paths
OS map	Explorer OL30 – Yorkshire Dales (Northern & Central Areas)
Refreshments	Coppice Café at national park visitor centre; Mill Race Teashop at Yore Mill
Toilets	At national park visitor centre
Parking	Aysgarth Falls Church Bank car park (pay and display)
Note	Stepping-stones across River Ure at Slapestone Wath will be impassable when river is in spate

Aysgarth Falls are a deservedly popular attraction, but relatively few people explore the wooded banks of the river just a little further downstream, which has equal charm. This route also wanders onto the higher ground to the north, across which is a fine view to nearby Castle Bolton, where the impressive ruin is open to visitors. The circuit can be conveniently linked to that of the previous walk to make a longer day and include an additional waterfall.

From the car park, stride down the lane and turn into **St Andrew's**. Walk through the churchyard past the southern front of the church, continuing across a small field beyond into a wood.

Emerging at the far side, keep going to join a broken wall at the edge of a high, wooded bank above the river. The **Lower Force** lies below you, and although you might get occasional glimpses of it through the trees, there is no access. However, you will have a grandstand view towards the end of the walk.

For the time being, carry on high above the water, eventually dropping to the riverbank, where the Ure spills out over a wide rocky bed. Climbing once more, the path leaves the river to run its course behind a curtain of trees, and hugs the edge of a couple of fields before turning across the final meadow to meet the main road by the entrance of **Hestholme Farm**. Follow the road over Hestholme Bridge, continuing around a bend to find a stile beside a gate on the left, from which a path is signed across the fields to Wensley Bridge.

The path strikes out across a couple of fields. Through a gate, bear left down through another gate into a small wood. The path winds through the trees above the confluence of **Bishopdale Beck** with the River Ure. Emerging at the far side, continue downstream beside the main river for another ¼ mile (400m) to reach a line of sturdy stepping-stones across the flow at **Slapestone Wath**. ▶

Having safely crossed, climb the bank and continue by the right-hand boundary, where a narrow old lane develops between flower-rich dilapidated walls and gnarled hedges. Towards the top, a slab bridge takes the path over a copious stream that originates from Kelder Well, springing from the ground in the fields above.

Meeting another track just beyond, **Thoresby Lane**, there is then a view north across the fields to the starkly impressive walls of Castle Bolton. To the left, the track continues through gates, eventually meeting a crossing.

Keep ahead passing below High Thoresby Farm, now following signs to Aysgarth. Beyond another gate, look for a stile breaking the right-hand wall, bringing a footpath from the farm. Do not go through, but instead bear left across the open pasture to find a stile near the far corner. Over that, keep by the left fence, emerging through a gate onto a track. Go left and keep left at a fork, following the track past **Hollins House**.

Just beyond the house, bear left to a field gate. The way falls gently ahead across

Warning If water is lapping over the stones, attempting a crossing is dangerous. If this is the case, retrace your steps to **Hestholme Bridge**, from where you can follow in reverse the route described in Walk 27, to see instead the waterfall at West Burton.

In the fields near Hollins House

parkland meadow to a gate at the far side. Carry on beside the boundary of St Joseph's Wood.

Planted out in 1999 with some 11,500 native trees, **St Joseph's Wood** has already become established as an important nature reserve. Together with the adjoining Freeholders' Wood, it attracts a wealth of wildlife, including roe deer, foxes and many birds. At dusk you might catch sight of a barn owl, while in spring you will certainly hear, if not see, drumming spotted woodpeckers.

Meeting a broad gravel track, double back left, soon dropping down steps to a viewing platform above the **Lower Force**. The path continues briefly upstream before climbing back to the main track, which to the left leads on beside the boundary of **Freeholders' Wood**. At a junction further on, more steps on the left descend to another viewpoint, this time overlooking the **Middle Force**.

Climb back to the path and follow it out to the edge of the wood, bearing right to leave through a gate onto

Aysgarth Lower Force

the lane. A short path opposite leads to the national park car park and **visitor centre**. Walk through the car park, where at the far end you will find another path that drops back to the road beside Yore Bridge. Access to the **Upper Falls** is through a gate on the right.

Returning to the road, cross the bridge to **Yore Mill**. Leave the road on the bend, passing beneath the balcony, and follow a stepped path into the churchyard. Walk through and retrace your steps to the car park.

WALK 29

Ivy Scar from Aysgarth

Start	Aysgarth National Park Visitor Centre (SE011887)
Distance	7 miles (11.3km)
Height gain	210m (689ft)
Time	2hr30
Terrain	Tracks and field paths
OS map	Explorer OL30 – Yorkshire Dales (Northern & Central Areas)
Refreshments	Coppice Café adjoining visitor centre, Mill Race Teashop at Yore Mill, the Wheatsheaf at Carperby
Toilets	Adjoining visitor centre
Parking	National park car park (pay and display)
Note	Stretches of riverside path may be impassable when the Ure is in spate

Wensleydale is known more for its history of dairy and sheep farming rather than industrial activity, but as elsewhere in the Dales, lead mining and quarrying were equally important undertakings, as revealed in this walk from Aysgarth. After following the course of the dismantled Wensleydale Railway to Woodhall, it climbs back across the slope of the hills to Carperby, where facets of this industrial heritage are to be found.

From the rear of the car park, a path drops left to meet the road beside **Yore Bridge**. Turning through a gate on the right, immediately before the bridge, follow a path past the entrance to the **Upper Falls** and picnic area.

After winding through trees, swing between the abutments of a dismantled railway bridge and strike left across the edge of **Bear Park**. Walk past a pair of copper beech trees to find a stile in the wall beyond, and go left, skirting the perimeter of the farm and big house, dropping beyond to come out onto its drive.

Cross to the stile opposite and head away at the edge of a couple of fields. Waymarks then divert you right and

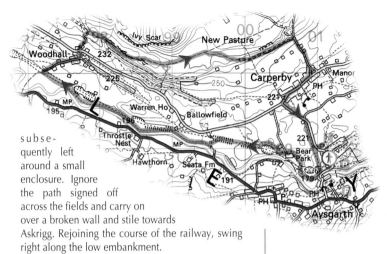

s u b s e-
quently left
around a small
enclosure. Ignore
the path signed off
across the fields and carry on
over a broken wall and stile towards
Askrigg. Rejoining the course of the railway, swing
right along the low embankment.

After passing above wetland meadows, where
reedy pools mark an ancient line of the river, the path
drops right down steps to a track. Still following signs
to Askrigg, go left between bridge abutments and then,
at a fork, bear right, crossing a stile into a riverside
meadow.

After crossing **Elter Beck**, the way continues
upstream beside lazy meanders of the river. Further up,
the Ure comes close to the embankment, squeezing the
path along a steep scrub bank. As the fields open out
beyond, the path remains by the right-hand wall.

Keep ahead beyond its end across a stream and, as
the river once more swings away, stay by the embankment. At the far end of the large field, cross a stile into
rough ground. Following a sign to **Woodhall**, go right and
take a track up past a farm into the hamlet. Later, keep left
at a fork and climb to a junction with the main lane.

Cross to a track beside a cottage opposite, which is
signed as a bridleway and winds up the field behind.
Where it splits, keep ahead to a gate in the top wall,
through which go right. The old way, known as **Ox Close
Road**, undulates easily across the hillside, giving a grand
view back across the valley, here dominated by the great
flat-topped hill of Addlebrough.

Along Wensleydale past Haw Bank

A short distance further on, it winds across **Thackwaite Beck** (which falls below the bridge over a small waterfall) and, through a field gate, continues at the edge of an expansive apron of meadow below **Ivy Scar**.

The hillside is richly veined with **lead ore**, and has been extensively mined in an industry that peaked during the 19th century. Just above the track, the power of Thackwaite Beck was harnessed with the construction of a small reservoir, while the cliffs a little further along are honeycombed with old adits and shafts, the ground below them heaped with piles of spoil.

More subtle are the **relics of earlier occupation**, seen in the vague boundary lines of ancient field systems. Towards the far end of the cliff, a circular ring of stones lying beside the track might mark a collapsed burial cairn, while a larger circular enclosure a little further on has been identified as a Bronze Age cremation cemetery.

Keep ahead where the gravel track swings towards the workings, gently rising in a shallow left arc to reach a gate in the top wall, **Oxclose Gate**. Through that, swing right and then curve within the corner of the wall to a second gate. Passing through, keep right, picking up a developing track that runs below a scar past old workings, from which great flags of stone were cut. ▶

Immediately beyond the workings, a bridleway drops between the fields to West End Farm and Carperby. However, the more pleasant route continues along the track below Ponderledge Scar for another ½ mile (800m) to meet an unsurfaced lane. It too leads down to Carperby, emerging at the eastern end of the village.

Business must have been bad when the quarries finally closed. It must have been uneconomic even to sell off the ready-cut stock – a great pile of flags still awaiting collection beside the track.

CARPERBY

Neatly laid out along a linear green, Carperby was one of the first villages in the Dales to be granted a market charter, which dates back to 1305. The stepped cross is inscribed with two dates, one from the 19th century recording its restoration, while the other, 1674, is thought to refer to a revival of the weekly event after competition from Askrigg.

Busy markets generally generate custom for several inns, but the village now has only one, the Wheatsheaf, which has been in business since the beginning of the 19th century. Amongst the Wheatsheaf's past guests were the honeymooners Mr and Mrs Alf Wight, who stayed here in November 1941. Since he combined his experiences as a country vet with a talent for storytelling, he is better known as James Herriot. A few weeks later, the hotel's guest book records another famous visitor, Greta Garbo, who came to entertain troops stationed at nearby Catterick.

Bear right to the main lane and there go right again, passing the village pub and a seven-stepped market cross.

At a junction on the edge of the village, turn left towards Aysgarth. After ¼ mile (400m), just after passing a narrow lane off left, look for a narrow gate into the field on the right. Signed to Aysgarth, the path at first tracks the wall beside the lane, but then entering parkland, bears away to go by a railed clump of trees.

Carry the line on down the hill, passing a couple of redundant stiles to reach a kissing-gate into a wood at the bottom. Cross the embankment of the old Wensleydale Railway and drop down steps back to the car park.

WALK 30
*Whitfield Gill Force and
Mill Gill Falls*

Start	Askrigg (SD947910)
Distance	3¼ miles (5.2km)
Height gain	200m (656ft)
Time	1hr30
Terrain	Field and rough woodland paths
OS map	Explorer OL30 – Yorkshire Dales (Northern & Central Areas)
Refreshments	Pubs and café in Askrigg
Toilets	At Askrigg
Parking	In village centre near the church (honesty box by church)

The walk climbs through the maze of grazing pastures above Askrigg to an old hill track, which leads to the head of the gorge of Whitfield Gill, the river that once powered the village's mills. Returning through the richly wooded valley, the path passes a couple of impressive waterfalls and reveals how the flow of water was harnessed for profit.

ASKRIGG

Sturdy and spaciously laid out, Askrigg has all the confidence of a prosperous country market town. Indeed it was granted a charter in 1587 but the name indicates its roots in a Norse settlement, 'the ridge where ash trees grow'. During the medieval period, the area was put to monastic sheep runs, and there was a small early monastery by the river just north of Bainbridge. Founded under Savigniac monastic rule, it was taken over by the Cistercians, who then moved to a new site at Jervaulx in the middle of the 12th century.

But it was not until the latter part of the 18th century that Askrigg really began to prosper, when the turnpike between Richmond and the port of Lancaster was routed through the town. The local industries of hand knitting, clock making, textiles and quarrying found new markets, bringing a wealth that is still reflected in the village's many fine buildings. However, the road, which followed the old Roman line from Bainbridge over the heights to Ribblehead, proved too hazardous in winter conditions, and in 1795 a more sheltered course was adopted through Hawes and along Widdale, the route still followed by the modern road. The focus of trade shifted to the market at Hawes, although Askrigg continued to benefit, particularly with the arrival of the railway in the higher dale around 1877.

Tucked away from the main road, Askrigg remains a lively and attractive village, neatly clustered around its 15th-century church, which is reputedly the biggest in the Dales. In the centre is a stone water pump and an impressive stepped cross, although this dates only from the 19th century.

Its popularity with visitors still owes much to its starring role as Darrowby in the much-loved TV dramatisation of James Herriot's All Creatures Great and Small, and fans will no doubt recognise 'Cringley House' and the 'Drovers Arms'.

From the market cross, follow the side street away beside **St Oswald's** churchyard. Just beyond a kinking double bend, look for a discreetly and retrospectively positioned sign indicating a footpath on the right along a house drive beside its garage. Entering the field behind, climb to the left corner and continue rising with the wall to a stile part-way up. Over that, cut left to a second one and carry on to a gap stile in the upper boundary.

Head up to a gate in the corner above a barn, and strike across an irregularly shaped field, making for a gated stile just below its upper left corner. Cross the corner up to another stile, and then climb up a final field to emerge, beside a gate at the top, onto a track, **Low Straights Lane**.

Follow the lane up the hill, to find a sign marking a path off to Mill Gill and Helm at the end. The path falls to the edge of a wooded gorge above **Whitfield Gill Force**, which at any time other than winter is heard rather than seen.

The path follows the rim downhill, eventually dropping steeply to a bridge spanning the stream above a small waterfall. Climb left to a junction, where a path leads back right above the gorge, a pleasant enough walk, but unfortunately offering little more of a view through the trees than before.

Return to the junction and continue down the valley. Breaking from the trees, keep ahead past a four-way signpost and through a stile, rising above the river beside a wall. At the crest, slip back into the wood, later reaching another signpost by a footbridge. Ignoring the bridge, swing right through the wall again to continue at the edge of fields above Mill Gill Fall.

Mill Gill Falls

Eventually, a gap stile leads back into the trees, the path running above the deep gorge before dropping past the ruin of an 18th-century lime kiln to a junction. The path doubling back this time really is worth the detour, and leads right to the foot of Mill Gill Falls.

> The foaming water of **Mill Gill Falls** spumes out of a narrow fissure in a single 20m drop to the pool below, which is thickly lined with ferns and lichen, well-drenched with the spray. Lime-rich water seeping from the rock has also formed the soft, porous rock called tufa. This has been a local beauty spot since Victorian times, when day-trippers would arrive by the railway and picnic here in the woods.

The path carries on down above the gorge, where a leat branches from the main flow of the river. Again the path momentarily deviates to the adjacent field before finally cutting back into the woods to a footbridge. On the other bank, wind out past one of the mills and continue on a flagged path across the meadow to meet the end of **Mill Lane**. Follow it back into the village.

> Mill Gill once powered three separate **mills** in the valley, which between them processed grain, or were involved in the spinning and dyeing of wool and, later, cotton. The mill past which the path leaves the wooded valley, its water conveyed in a high-level galvanised conduit, began life as a grist mill, but in the early 20th century was harnessed to run a dynamo, producing electricity for the village.

WALK 31
*The Wensleydale railway and
River Ure stepping-stones*

Start	Bainbridge (SD934901)
Distance	3½ miles (5.6km)
Height gain	80m (262ft)
Time	1hr15
Terrain	Tracks and field paths
OS map	Explorer OL30 – Yorkshire Dales (Northern & Central Areas)
Refreshments	Cornmill Tearoom and Rose and Crown Hotel at Bainbridge
Toilets	Beside village green
Parking	Roadside parking around village green (donations)
Note	Stepping-stones across the River Ure at Borwins will be impassable when the river is in spate, in which case follow Walk 32.

The former Wensleydale Railway closely dogged the course of the river from Aysgarth all the way up to its junction with the main Settle–Carlisle line at Garsdale, and would have made a fine recreation trail along the valley after its complete closure in 1964. Unfortunately, the opportunity was missed. However, some short sections are followed by footpaths, the one exploited here being along the northern bank of the river west from Bainbridge. After crossing the water on sturdy stepping-stones, the return route rises along the hillside to Greensley Bank. There, you can either cut across to the Cam High Road to extend the walk out to Semer Water, detailed in the next walk, or simply drop in a leisurely fashion back through the fields to the village.

BAINBRIDGE

Bainbridge's history hails back to the eighth decade of the first century, when the Romans, under the Emperor Agricola, established a small strategic fort atop a high drumlin set back from the Ure overlooking River Bain. Apart from a short period during the second century, it was garrisoned right until the departure of the Romans from Britain in AD410. The outline of its defences remains clearly visible from the hillside behind the village.

With the arrival of the Normans in northern England, large tracts of Wensleydale were reserved as hunting forest. A relic of those days can be seen in the Rose and Crown – a horn that was blown at the end of each day to guide foresters and travellers back to the village. The tradition is still maintained, with the horn being blown at 10.00 each evening from the end of September until Shrove Tuesday.

Head out from the village along the road to Askrigg, which drops from the green by the Rose and Crown Hotel and leads past the **Friends' Meeting House**.

FRIENDS' MEETING HOUSE

Built in 1836, the Friends' Meeting House replaced an old cottage in the village that had previously been used for meetings by the Quakers in the dale since 1668. Adjoining it is a burial ground, where amongst the graves are to be found the resting places of Alexander Fothergill, who was responsible for laying out along the valley the course of the Richmond to Lancaster turnpike, opened in 1751, and Richard Robinson, who lived at Countersett Hall, and was one of George Fox's first converts in the dale.

George Fox founded the 'Friends of Truth', which subsequently became known as the Society of Friends, or Quakers. Fox came from Fenny Drayton in Leicestershire, but spent much time travelling and preaching in the north of England. Shortly after experiencing a vision on Pendle Hill, in which he saw a multitude coming to Christ, he preached to a gathering of over a thousand people on Firbank Fell outside Sedbergh, and gained many converts in the area.

Stepping-stones at Borwins

Warning Attempting passage when the river is in flood is dangerous, in which case either simply retrace your steps to Bainbridge or, alternatively, go back to the junction by the bridge abutment and join Walk 32 to return via Skell Gill.

Immediately after crossing the river at **Yore Bridge**, leave through a squeeze stile on the left and bear up the bank to join the former bed of the railway through a kissing-gate. Follow its course above the river for nearly 1¼ miles (2km), eventually passing below a large house at Hill Top and winding right to a junction of tracks.

Guided by a sign to Middle Borwins, swing left and left again between the abutments of a dismantled railway bridge and then go right at the field edge past a barn. Carry on beside a paddock to a small gate by a lean-to. Following waymarks, move left through a larger gate into an enclosure and cross to a gate on the left. Head down a meadow to **stepping-stones** across the river. ◀

However, if the stepping-stones are safe, cross to the far bank and bear left to a gate around the corner of the wall above. Go forward, and then right past a farmhouse to meet its access track, following it away to the main road.

Cross to a track opposite, signed as a footpath to Greensley Bank, which winds gently upwards across the hillside.The increasing height opens a vista across the dale to the northern hills of Stags Fell and Askrigg

Common, although the river itself is obscured behind the low, green-backed glacial humps that rumple the valley floor.

Reaching the farm at **Greensley Bank** there is a choice of paths. To join the walk to Semer Water (Walk 33), peel off right just before the farm, dropping through a dip to a gate in a wall. Continue the same line up to the distant top corner of the field to gain the **Cam High Road**.

Otherwise, to return to the village, carry on through the yard past the house and leave through a gate at its far end. Head across the fields, losing height to pass right of a small barn. Cross the stream falling below, and follow it briefly down before being forced away by a wall.

Keep ahead to the far side of the next large field and there, through a couple of narrow gates, pass above another barn. With the village now in sight ahead, continue towards it across the remaining fields, emerging past a small car park and the Yoredale offices of the national park. Reaching the street beyond, turn left back to the village centre.

WALK 32

The Wensleydale railway and Skell Gill

Start	Bainbridge (SD934901)
Distance	5½ miles (8.9km)
Height gain	175m (574ft)
Time	2hr
Terrain	Tracks and field paths
OS map	Explorer OL30 – Yorkshire Dales (Northern & Central Areas)
Refreshments	Cornmill Tearoom and Rose and Crown Hotel at Bainbridge
Toilets	Beside village green
Parking	Roadside parking around village green (donations)

A fine walk in its own right, this route, which contours the fringe of Cote Pasture to Skell Gill, also offers an alternative return to Bainbridge for Walk 31 if the stepping-stones at Cams are impassable.

PASTURE AND FLOWER MEADOWS

Grass grown as pasture or to produce hay and silage is one of the country's largest farming crops – particularly so in the Dales, where sheep and cattle form the mainstay of most farms. In the drive for greater productivity, many old pastures and meadows have been tilled and re-seeded, but in the Dales a significant number of pastures and meadows remain, abundant in wildflowers, herbs and sweet grass species. They are not only a feast for the eyes in early summer, but give Wensleydale cheese its unique richness and flavour.

Looking across Cote Pasture to Whitfield Scar

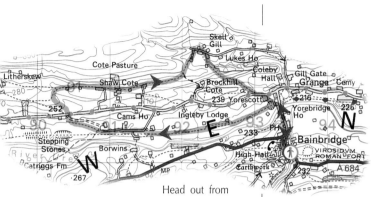

Head out from Bainbridge along the road to Askrigg, which drops from the green by the Rose and Crown Hotel and leads past the **Friends' Meeting House** to the River Yore.

Immediately after crossing the river at **Yore Bridge**, leave through a squeeze stile on the left and bear up the bank to join the former bed of the railway through a kissing-gate. Follow its course above the river for nearly 1¼ miles (2km), eventually passing below a large house at **Hill Top** and winding right to a junction of tracks.

Looking beyond Skell Gill to Whitfield Scar

Across Wensleydale to Addlebrough

Go left and keep ahead past the dismantled abutments of bridge to a stile. Keep going at the field edge to emerge through a kissing gate onto a lane. Follow it left.

At the end by **Old Cams House** and Barn, swing right with the track. Immediately over a cattle-grid, bear off left across rough pasture following a sign to Litherskew. Rising across a bank, pick up a grass track that leads out to the main lane. Cross to a gate opposite, from which another green track is signed half-left across the hillside to Sedbusk. Winding to a gate in the top wall, the way continues as a walled track. Keep going by the right-hand wall beyond its end towards **Shaw Cote**. A permissive path skirts above the farm before returning you to the field edge. Carry on across the hillside towards Skell Gill, later passing a second farm.

After another 400m, passing a waypost, the path moves away from the wall, rising over the shoulder of the hill to a signpost beside another wall. Follow it down left towards Skell Gill, dropping through a gate along a walled track. At a junction, go right, passing a cottage to reach an old bridge across **Skellgill Beck**.

At a signpost immediately before the bridge, turn off through a gate on the right towards Breconbar. Follow the field edge down beside the stream, shortly passing through a gate in the corner by a laithe. Bear right, climbing to a gate in the top wall and continue the same diagonal line down the next field. Eventually closing with the left wall, keep going to emerge over a stile onto a lane.

Go left to **Yorescott**, leaving there through a signposted stile on the right. Cut left in front of the farmhouse to a second stile and strike out on a diagonal line across the crest of the field, dropping to the kissing-gate beside the old railway track followed on the way out. Retrace your steps back to Bainbridge.

LAITHES

One of Wensleydale's many field barns

One of the ubiquitous and most attractive features of the Dales farming landscape is the proliferation of laithes or field barns scattered across the valley fields. Throughout the medieval period and beyond, these were cruck barns constructed of timber and thatch, and consequently very few examples have survived. The 18th century brought a gradual revolution in farming, with field enclosure and improved practices bringing greater productivity and prosperity. This in turn saw stone being used for more than just churches and castles. The barns served both to store fodder and overwinter stock and by siting them at intervals among the meadows, much time and effort was saved both in harvesting the hay and dispersing the manure back onto the fields.

WALK 33

Bainbridge to Semer Water

Start	Bainbridge (SD934901)
Distance	5½ miles (8.9km)
Height gain	300m (984ft)
Time	2hr15
Terrain	Tracks and field paths
OS map	Explorer OL30 – Yorkshire Dales (Northern & Central Areas)
Refreshments	Cornmill Tearoom, and Rose and Crown Hotel at Bainbridge
Toilets	Beside village green
Parking	Roadside parking around village green (donations)

In a fold of the valley above the village lies Semer Water, noted as one of only two natural lakes of any significance in the whole of the Dales. The lake is drained by the River Bain, which also claims fame as the shortest river in England, a mere two miles (3.2km) from its source to being lost in the River Ure. This splendid circuit explores both, and throws in a Roman road as well. For a longer day, this walk can be tacked onto the ramble by the River Ure (Walk 31).

From the southern end of the village, where the main road to Aysgarth leaves, take the short street past the **Cornmill Tearoom**, which is signed as a footpath to the River Bain. Fork right in front of Beech House, and keep ahead along the edge of the front yard of a house to a small gate in the corner. Climb away, following the perimeter of a couple of fields before parting company with the wall as it later turns away. Continue above a steep-sided bank that falls to the river.

Carry on, passing below a barn, and then aim for the top corner of the next field. Keep going across a couple more fields and an intervening stream, emerging just right of a house at the top of the hill, **Gill Edge**. Walk out to the lane and stroll downhill to the second bend, where you will find a track signed off as a bridleway to Beggerman's Road.

It is at this point that the route of the previous walk joins from Greensley Bank. Marked as the **Cam High Road** on the Ordnance Survey map, the track climbs away dead straight along the slope of the hill.

> The track follows the line of a **Roman road** that ran from the fort at Bainbridge across the Dales, past Ingleton to Bentham, where it met the Western Way, the main link between Ribchester and Carlisle. In the middle of the 18th century, it was incorporated within the Richmond to Lancaster turnpike, but the route proved too demanding in the harsh conditions of winter, and in 1795 it was re-routed further along the valley to Hawes, where it climbed to Ribblehead along Widdale, the course still used today.

After 1¼ miles (2km), look for unmarked gap stiles, first on the left and then on the right-hand side of the track. Should you find yourself meeting a fell road, you have gone a little too far, but no matter, you can simply follow it up the hill. If you do spot the stiles, go through the one on the left and strike a left diagonal, climbing the rough pasture on a vague trod to intercept the lane higher up.

Go left to the crest, leaving immediately beyond through a gate on the bend. Turn right in the field and follow the wall down the hillside. Over a stile at

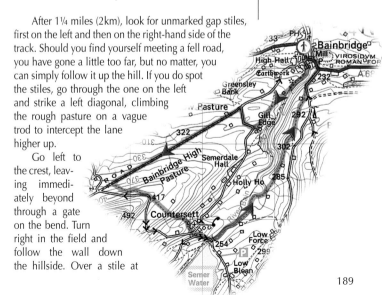

189

the bottom, Semer Water suddenly pops into view, the way continuing towards it through a grassy notch. As the ground opens out below, bear left, aiming for a small barn in the adjacent field.

Crossing a stile just before it, turn right down to a stream and stile. Beyond, wayposts guide you across a final field to leave beside cottages next to **Countersett Hall**. Emerging onto a lane, go right and then left, the way signed to Stalling Busk, and dropping steeply to **Semer Water Bridge** at the foot of the lake.

COUNTERSETT HALL

Countersett Hall was the home of Richard Robinson, one of the first converts in the valley to the 'Friends of the Truth' – the Quakers. Isolated from the mainstream of life, and enduring an often-harsh existence, many Dales folk found little relevance to their lives in the dogma of the established church. The sentiments preached by George Fox struck a chord, however, and he gained many followers among those who came to listen to him speak during his visits to the area. Despite persecution for his faith, and imprisonment for refusing to pay tithes to the Church, Robinson held meetings at the hall, and his son Michael subsequently founded a separate meeting house, still in use today.

By walking just a little further, you can get down to the lake shore.

An erratic boulder at the edge of Semer Water

SEMER WATER

One of the fascinations of the English countryside is that almost everywhere you go, the richness of the scene is enhanced with the colour of a host of folk tales woven into the tapestry. The intermixing of imagination with taboo and half-remembered history, and the attempt to explain the mysteries of nature, has created a lavish legacy of stories that still have the power to stir a romantic soul. Semer Water, one of only two natural lakes of any size in the Yorkshire Dales, is no exception, with a legend of a lost village drowned beneath its waters.

A beggar travelling through the valley on a stormy night sought shelter at the village in the dale, but was spurned at every cottage save one, that of a poor widow, who offered him food and drink. Continuing upon his way, he looked back at the inhospitable place and uttered a curse: 'Simmerwater rise and Simmerwater sink, drown all save the house of the poor woman that gave me drink'. The rising waters engulfed the village, leaving just the one cottage on the shore. That building too has now gone, but it is said that its stones were used for the bridge, and when the waters are very low, perhaps you might just make out the drowned village.

Modern science, however, reveals that the waters of the lake were trapped by moraine debris left by retreating glaciation at the end of the last ice age. Issuing from its northern tip is reputedly the shortest river in the country, which flows down to join the Ure at Bainbridge. But during heavy rain the lake cannot cope with the influx from the three separate valleys that feed it, and the water rises dramatically to flood the banks, no doubt contributing to the inspiration of the tale.

The return, however, lies through a gate on the left, immediately over the bridge. A riverside path, signed to Blean Lane and Bainbridge, passes through successive pastures for a good ½ mile (800m), eventually reaching a ladder stile. Over that, leave the river and bear right towards the higher ground, making for a stile in the end wall. Keep ahead across a couple of fields, before the way begins to climb towards the top of **Bracken Hill**. ▸ Over the crest, the route falls through a squeeze stile and heads gently down above the river, which by now is confined within a narrow, deep gorge. Passing an oddly rectangular enclosure and tall narrow barn, the path curves left in more earnest descent beside the wall bounding a lane.

Although of only modest height, the hill is a superb vantage point, with views ahead past Virosidum, the Roman fort, across the river to Askrigg, and behind, to the higher reaches of Raydale beyond Semer Water.

The Rose and Crown at Bainbridge

Emerging at the bottom onto the main road, turn left back into the village, re-crossing the River Bain as it escapes its constriction, tumbling over a succession of broad slabs in final exuberance before being lost in the River Ure just a ¼ mile (400m) to the north.

WALK 34
Aysgill Force

Start	Hawes (SD875898)
Distance	4¼ miles (6.8km)
Height gain	150m (492ft)
Time	1hr45
Terrain	Tracks and field paths
OS maps	Explorer OL2 – Yorkshire Dales (Southern & Western Areas) or Explorer OL30 – Yorkshire Dales (Northern & Central Areas)
Refreshments	Pubs and cafés in Hawes
Toilets	Beside car park
Parking	National park car park (pay and display)

This undemanding stroll is a popular local walk, following Gayle Beck into the lower reaches of Sleddale, where there is a small but arresting waterfall. It lies in a wooded section of the valley, and during high summer the trees can partly obscure the view. But set within a charming and peaceful corner, it is nevertheless worthy of investigation at any time of the year.

Leaving the Hawes car park, turn right along the main road, and bear left to follow the one-way system through the town centre. As the roads come together again, swing off left beside a shop at a Pennine Way signpost along a covered ginnel and climb beside **St Margaret's Church**. Through a gate at the top, a path continues across a couple of fields behind the **Wensleydale Creamery** to meet a road on the edge of **Gayle**.

Go left into the village, bending left again at the top towards the bridge. Just before crossing,

turn down a narrow cobbled path fronting riverside cottages, and keep ahead as it then opens into a street. Just after the last house on the left, climb steps to a kissing-gate into the field behind.

Bear right with a trod, climbing to a stile in the far wall. Following a sign to Aysgill Force, continue half-left towards the far corner of the next pasture. To the left is a good view across the foot of Sleddale to Wether Fell, while Dodd Fell Hill rises at the head of the valley.

Through a squeeze style, a stepped path drops across a wooded bank towards the river. Carry on upstream from meadow to meadow, crossing a sloping bank and later re-entering the wooded fringe before shortly arriving at **Aysgill Force**.

The stream generally flows placidly over a rounded stubby nose of tufa to a dark pool some 10m below the lip, but in full flood after heavy rain can present an altogether different and spectacular sight. The steep banks prevent you getting down to see the fall from the bottom, but the river is more accessible above, where the water simply drops from view. However, do not approach the lip too closely, for the rocks are slippery.

Beyond the fall, the path breaks from the trees and continues past a footbridge to rejoin the field edge. At a second footbridge by a barn, again carry on by the waterside, but in the next field, the river moves away left, the path continuing ahead to intercept a rough track at the far side. Turn right, passing out through a gate onto another track and go right again.

The track runs on for almost a mile (1.6km), passing through a farmyard and later swinging left to become **Mossy Lane**. Carry on ahead for a further 600m to find a path signed off right across a succession of fields back to Hawes. It emerges onto the road at the edge of Gayle by the Wensleydale Creamery. Return to **Hawes** by way of your outward path, which lies beyond the creamery to the right.

Crossing rough pastures in Sleddale

HAWES

Hawes is renowned for its creamery, producing Wensleydale cheese, continuing a tradition begun by monks from Savigny in France when they established a monastery at Fors around 1145. The site proved too remote, however, and the community decamped to a better location further down the valley at Jervaulx, which flourished until Henry's dissolution. However, their distinctive cheese continued to be made on local farms, and in 1897 was first produced on a commercial scale here at Hawes. The dairy has suffered a few hiccups since then, and at one point was closed, with cheese production being transferred to Lancashire, adding more than insult to injury. In 1992, however, a management buy-out returned the business to its rightful home, and you can now visit the museum, watch cheese being made from the viewing gallery and, of course, buy some to take home.

WALK 35
Dodd Fell Hill and Drumaldrace

Start	Hawes (SD875898)
Distance	11½ miles (18.5km)
Height gain	570m (1870ft)
Time	4hr45
Terrain	Upland tracks, some pathless moorland
OS maps	Explorer OL2 – Yorkshire Dales (Southern & Western Areas) and Explorer OL30 – Yorkshire Dales (Northern & Central Areas)
Refreshments	Pubs and cafés in Hawes
Toilets	Beside car park
Parking	National park car park (pay and display)
Note	Dogs are not allowed on Open Access land away from rights of way

The two summits linked in this horseshoe around the head of Sleddale are invariably ignored by the many walkers who follow the ancient, well-trodden routes across their flanks. Yet, despite the lack of obvious paths across the tussock moor onto the tops, they are easily reached, and in clear weather afford superb viewpoints across upper Wensleydale.

Leaving the car park, go right and then bear left, following the one-way street system into the town centre. Just before the roads come together again, swing left and climb a narrow ginnel beside **St Margaret's Church**. Through a gate at the top, a path continues across pastures behind the **Wensleydale Creamery** to emerge at the edge of **Gayle**.

Turn left into the village, bending towards the bridge, but leave the road immediately before it down a narrow cobbled path past a row of riverside cottages. Continue along the street beyond to find, just after the last house on the left, a footpath signed off up steps to a kissing-gate.

GAYLE

Straddling the beck at the foot of Sleddale, Gayle was always distinct from Hawes, and until the 17th century was more important than its neighbour. Outcropping coal and sound rock supported mining and quarrying, which, together with a flourishing hand-knitting industry, bolstered meagre incomes from farming.

The development of the turnpike in the latter part of the 18th century brought fresh enterprise, with the construction of a mill to spin cotton, imported from the newly independent America by way of Lancaster. The mill was later used to spin flax and then wool before being converted to a sawmill and carpentry. In the early 20th century, a generator was also installed to produce electricity. The business closed in 1988, but the mill has since reopened as a museum, offering a fascinating insight into the way in which the power of the stream has been harnessed for industry over the centuries.

Bear right across the field to meet the Pennine Way at a stile and follow it ahead across more fields to a narrow lane. Go right and then left onto a gravel track, **Gaudy Lane**, which begins the steady ascent onto the high ground. Approaching **Gaudy Farm**, abandon the track over a stile beside a gate on the left. Sticking with the right wall, continue up the hill, the way now signed to Ten End.

Cottongrass dances in the breeze above Gaudy House

Passing through a gate, the unwavering path trudges gently upwards. Over to the right is Widdale, a pretty valley that carries the road south over the watershed to another Gayle, and on to Ribblehead, while on the other side is Wether Fell, over which the route ultimately returns to Hawes. Beyond its foot, Wensleydale stretches into the distance, overshadowed by the distinctive profile of Addlebrough.

Higher up, the path balks at the steepening gradient and adopts an easier line along the flank. The transition to limestone is heralded by a lime kiln and a line of shake holes before the path climbs onto the peaty layers of **Ten End**.

Cam Road, an ancient muleteer's track, joins from below, taking the way on above the closed valley of Snaizeholme. Beyond a gate the accompanying wall soon ends, but Cam Road runs on, more or less level, across the northwestern flank of Dodd Fell Hill.

The way to the summit, however, lacks any sort of a path, and you must make the best way you can across rough tussock. Either bear left off the track just beyond the end of the wall and head due south or carry on for another ½ mile (800m) along the track and then strike up east.

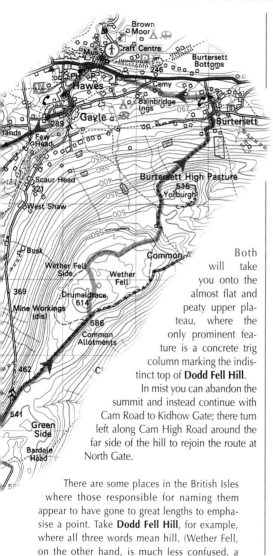

Both will take you onto the almost flat and peaty upper plateau, where the only prominent feature is a concrete trig column marking the indistinct top of **Dodd Fell Hill**.

In mist you can abandon the summit and instead continue with Cam Road to Kidhow Gate; there turn left along Cam High Road around the far side of the hill to rejoin the route at North Gate.

There are some places in the British Isles where those responsible for naming them appear to have gone to great lengths to emphasise a point. Take **Dodd Fell Hill**, for example, where all three words mean hill. (Wether Fell, on the other hand, is much less confused, a wether simply being a castrated ram.) What the top lacks in character is compensated for in the reward of a far-flung panorama across this corner of the Dales. To the north is Great Shunner Fell flanked by Lovely Seat, while to the south, Yorkshire's Three Peaks can be seen. The next top, Drumaldrace on Wether Fell, beckons to the northeast, but as Sleddale intervenes, you must take a roundabout route.

Walk from the trig pillar on a southeasterly bearing, an intermittent trod now serving as a guide. The path soon begins to lose height towards the peaty gathering grounds heading Sleddale, where you should keep your line across and avoid being drawn into the valley.

In front, the eye is attracted to Oughtershaw and Langstrothdale, a long and lovely valley nurturing the infant River Wharfe. Picking through the hags, the loping descent leads to a wall, whose convoluted course you should then follow to the left, ultimately meeting Cam High Road at **North Gate**.

Cam High Road was once a **Roman thoroughfare** that ran between Bainbridge and Ingleton, and which continued in use throughout the Middle Ages. In the 18th century it was incorporated within the Richmond to Lancaster turnpike. But winter conditions on the upper sections, where it runs for more than three miles (4.8km) at over 550m, proved too much, and in 1795 a new road was opened along Widdale.

Go left, eventually joining the fell road between Gayle and Langstrothdale and follow it downhill for ½ mile (800m). As the lane suddenly drops away, branch off onto a byway continuing the line of the old Roman road to Bainbridge across Wether Fell.

Gently climbing, the view along Sleddale is superseded by the appearance of Rydale, where there is a glimpse of Semer Water as the track crests the rise. After almost a mile (1.6km) the left wall turns away, the bridle-way signed beside it offering a poor-weather alternative.

The way over **Drumaldrace**, however, follows a wandering upwards trod to find a small pile of stones marking the high point. Although some 50m lower than Dodd Fell Hill, a changed perspective reveals equally satisfying views – beyond Widdale is Baugh Fell, with Swarth Fell and Wild Boar Fell to its right.

Of the several trods radiating from the cairn, take the one heading north, which weaves between the low peat hags of the plateau, and falls to meet the clearer and better-footed encircling bridleway by a kink in the wall.

To the right, it curves around the northern upper slopes of Wether Fell, passing a small abandoned quarry and leading to a gate. Beyond, the way develops as a track, winding down to a gap in a long wall by a ram-shackle shed. The continuing track drops through the lower pastures, ultimately coming out onto a back street in **Burtersett**.

Go right and then left to follow the main lane into the village, looking for the former Wesleyan Methodist Chapel, now converted to a dwelling. Turn beside it

The tiny hamlet of Burtersett

along a ginnel signed to Hawes, from which an old flagged path runs across a succession of hay meadows.

Eventually reaching a lane, cross diagonally left to the ongoing path, which soon closes behind a row of houses. Emerging onto the main road, head left back into the town.

The northern flank of Drumaldrace rises behind Gayle

WALK 36
Cotterdale

Start	Hardraw (SD866911)
Distance	7 miles (11.3km)
Height gain	360m (1181ft)
Time	3hr
Terrain	Upland paths and tracks
OS map	Explorer OL19 – Howgill Fells & Upper Eden Valley
Refreshments	Cart House Craft & Tea Shop and the Green Dragon Inn at Hardraw
Toilets	None
Parking	Roadside parking at western edge of Hardraw (donations)

Much of the enjoyment of the walk onto Great Shunner Fell derives from the expansive views it reveals. But when the mist is down, the secluded valley of Cotterdale nestling beneath its southern flank provides an enjoyable alternative. This route shares some of that used during the return from the top of the hill in Walk 37, but is here employed in the opposite direction, and thus presents a completely different perspective across the dale.

HARDRAW FORCE

The walk begins from the tiny village of Hardraw, famous for its falls, which lie behind the Green Dragon Inn. The entry charge supports the maintenance of the site. Besides a heritage centre illustrating its history, you can follow many of the paths originally laid out for the Victorian tourists.

The natural amphitheatre of the gorge is still the venue for the annual September brass band concert, first held in 1884, and the pub has become a focus for music with the Gathering every July and other festivals and impromptu sessions taking place throughout the year.

The waterfall, which dominates the head of the gorge, comprises the highest single-drop cascade in England, the water plummeting over 30m straight down from the lip. It is seen at its best after heavy rain, when the thundering torrent crashes to the pool at the base of the cliff. Yet in the depths of a hard winter frost it can be frozen into awe-inspiring immobility.

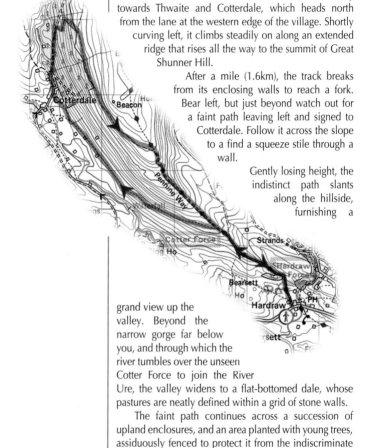

Take the farm track marked as the Pennine Way towards Thwaite and Cotterdale, which heads north from the lane at the western edge of the village. Shortly curving left, it climbs steadily on along an extended ridge that rises all the way to the summit of Great Shunner Hill.

After a mile (1.6km), the track breaks from its enclosing walls to reach a fork. Bear left, but just beyond watch out for a faint path leaving left and signed to Cotterdale. Follow it across the slope to a find a squeeze stile through a wall.

Gently losing height, the indistinct path slants along the hillside, furnishing a grand view up the valley. Beyond the narrow gorge far below you, and through which the river tumbles over the unseen Cotter Force to join the River Ure, the valley widens to a flat-bottomed dale, whose pastures are neatly defined within a grid of stone walls.

The faint path continues across a succession of upland enclosures, and an area planted with young trees, assiduously fenced to protect it from the indiscriminate nibbling of sheep. Eventually crossing a stile in the lower wall above a short ravine from which springs **Robin Rash**

In the forest above Cotterdale

Well, the path slants through rougher, wetter ground, emerging at the bottom over a stream and another stile into the lower meadows.

Keep ahead towards the hamlet, passing out at the far side of the third field over a footbridge spanning **East Gill** onto a lane. Follow it right through the tiny hamlet of **Cotterdale**.

COTTERDALE

The handful of sturdy cottages, some dating to the beginning of the 17th century, housed a small farming community that supplemented its income by digging coal out of the hill above and knitting, a cottage industry carried out in many of the dales. Ignored by the main road, it has an air of remoteness and preserves much of its old character.

Joining the river above the village, continue past a bridge bringing a track out of the forest to a second bridge, just upstream. On the far bank, swing right to find a small gate, through which a path climbs beside a pretty wooded stream to meet a broad forest track higher up.

Continue up the hill along the main winding track, taking note at each fork of the signposts that identify the course of the bridleway. Three-quarters of a mile (1.2km) of steady ascent brings you to the upper boundary of the plantation, the track rising a little distance beyond to meet a rough crossing track.

Follow the track right above the perimeter of the trees, chasing an intermittent line of shake holes that marks the edge of a bed of limestone. Beyond the trees the way begins gradually to gain height across the hillside, shortly passing through a gate.

Carry on for another easy ¾ mile (1.2km) to join the Pennine Way descending the spine of the hill. This will take you back down to Hardraw, some 1¾ miles (2.8km) away, picking up your outward route lower down.

WALK 37

Great Shunner Fell from Hardraw

Start	Hardraw (SD866911)
Distance	10½ miles (16.9km)
Height gain	555m (1821ft)
Time	4hr15
Terrain	Moorland paths
OS map	Explorer OL19 – Howgill Fells & Upper Eden Valley
Refreshments	Cart House Craft & Tea Shop and Green Dragon Inn at Hardraw
Toilets	None
Parking	Roadside parking at western edge of Hardraw (donations)
Note	Dogs are not allowed on Open Access land away from rights of way

Unless you are prepared for a long tramp across largely trackless moors, or are fortunate in your transport arrangements, Great Shunner Fell is usually treated as a 'there and back' walk, either from Thwaite or Hardraw. However, from Hardraw there is the opportunity to vary the return via Cotterdale, a quiet valley wherein snuggles an unspoilt hamlet overlooking flat valley-bottom fields. In fact, such is Cotterdale's appeal that it offers a respectable lower-level walk in its own right, which is described in Walk 36.

Great Shunner Fell, at 716m, is the third highest of the Yorkshire Dales peaks, subordinate only to Whernside and Ingleborough. It is a massive moorland hill, and being well detached from its neighbours, both in terms of distance and re-ascent, offers a magnificent distant panorama across the surrounding fells.

Its long and well-graded spine carries the Pennine Way between Wensleydale and Swaledale, a generally good and clear track throughout, which helps boost its popularity with both distance and

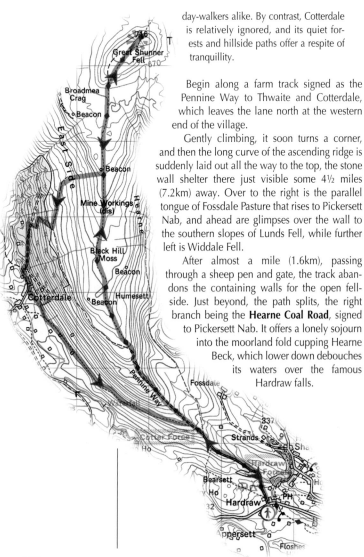

day-walkers alike. By contrast, Cotterdale is relatively ignored, and its quiet forests and hillside paths offer a respite of tranquillity.

Begin along a farm track signed as the Pennine Way to Thwaite and Cotterdale, which leaves the lane north at the western end of the village.

Gently climbing, it soon turns a corner, and then the long curve of the ascending ridge is suddenly laid out all the way to the top, the stone wall shelter there just visible some 4½ miles (7.2km) away. Over to the right is the parallel tongue of Fossdale Pasture that rises to Pickersett Nab, and ahead are glimpses over the wall to the southern slopes of Lunds Fell, while further left is Widdale Fell.

After almost a mile (1.6km), passing through a sheep pen and gate, the track abandons the containing walls for the open fellside. Just beyond, the path splits, the right branch being the **Hearne Coal Road**, signed to Pickersett Nab. It offers a lonely sojourn into the moorland fold cupping Hearne Beck, which lower down debouches its waters over the famous Hardraw falls.

▶ The way to the top, however, keeps with the Pennine Way along the left branch, continuing as an easy but unremitting plod. Ignore the footpath shortly signed off left to Cotterdale and stay with the main track.

The great emptiness of the sweeping moor is relieved by nothing more than a couple of remote barns, its stillness broken only by the sound of skylarks, curlew and golden plover.

Another mile (1.6km) of easy walking culminates in a sharper pull past the rubble of old quarry workings. Just beyond, through a gate is another signpost, where the Pennine Way is now marked off to the right.

The way narrows but remains clear, becoming more rugged and occasionally wet, but the worst bits are avoided by a flagged path, laid in 1996 to alleviate the erosion created by increasing numbers of feet tramping the long-distance path.

After a further 1½ miles (2.4km) the hill buckles in another rise at **Crag End**. Take note of a faint path leaving on the left at the foot of the pull, for it marks the route down to Cotterdale, should you decide later to

Hearne Coal Road led, as its name suggests, to coal mines below Pickersett Edge, which were worked into the early years of the last century. This is one of several places around the hill where accessible coal seams outcrop.

The stone windbreak on top of Great Shunner Fell

The old coal road on the lower slopes of Great Shunner Fell

return that way. For the time being, however, carry on for another mile, the way occasionally squirming through hags before finally breaking onto firmer ground for the final run across a stile in an intervening fence to the summit of **Great Shunner Fell**.

The wide-ranging view stretches west past the Howgills to the distant Lakeland hills, and to the south are the famous Three Peaks that bound the head of Ribblesdale – Whernside, Ingleborough and Pen-y-ghent. Over to the southeast the ground dips across the head of the Buttertubs pass to Lovely Seat, while to the northwest, on a really clear day you can see all the way to Cross Fell, 25 miles (40km) distant.

Retrace your steps to **Crag End**, the rubble cairn above the steepening slope being all that remains of a pillar beacon, similar to the Long Gill Beacon, seen earlier over to the right.

If you are short of time, you can simply retrace your steps to Hardraw, but otherwise leave the main path just below the cairn and head out right across the moor to pick up a reasonably evident green track dropping from the ridge towards the upper valley of Cotterdale.

Quickly losing height, the way passes between grassed heaps marking old coal workings, some piles of shale still defying the encroachment of vegetation after nearly a century. Reaching a more distinct grass track lower down, follow it left, shortly meeting a gravel track rising out of an area of conifer plantation.

Follow the track down, observing the fingerposts at successive junctions that will keep you on course. Before reaching the bottom edge of the plantation area, look for a signed grass path forking off right that drops beside a stream to emerge from the plantation past a small picnic area. Through a gate the path winds right to a bridge across **East Gill** and then follows it downstream, over a crossing track into the hamlet of **Cotterdale**.

Just past cottages on the left, keep an eye open for a path signed to Hardraw over a footbridge. Bear right across the field towards a gap stile in the far wall and continue over the fields. Leaving the third field over a stile and stream, continue across the rougher pasture of the hillside, gradually closing with the upper wall.

Beyond a stile above the head of a small ravine, the ongoing trod, occasionally marked by wayposts, continues across the hillside. The way keeps its height as it passes through successive enclosures, one of which has been fenced off and planted with trees.

Eventually, it slants upwards to gain the shoulder of the falling ridge, meeting your outward track from Hardraw. It is then an easy mile down the hill back into the village.

WALK 38
The High Way

Start	Shaw Paddock on B6259, ¾ mile (1.2km) south of national park boundary (SD784952)
Distance	5¼ miles (8.4km)
Height gain	205m (673ft)
Time	2hr
Terrain	Moorland tracks and field trods
OS map	Explorer OL19 – Howgill Fells & Upper Eden Valley
Refreshments	The Moorcock Inn – 1¾ miles (2.8km) south of Shaw Paddock
Toilets	None
Parking	Small lay-by north of railway bridge

The high moorland slopes of Lunds Fell give birth to two main river systems – the River Eden, which runs north to enter the Solway Firth beyond Carlisle, and the River Ure, which manages two changes of identity before finally slipping past Spurn Head into the North Sea. Although not climbing all the way up the hill to the actual sources, this walk crosses the head streams of both in their early stages, following the line of an ancient track. Its course traces the contour of an outcropping band of limestone across the hillside, and in addition to affording fine views across the heads of the three valleys that meet here, reveals many subtle features of karst landscape.

The walk begins from the B6259 at Shaw Paddock, where there is parking for a couple of cars just north of the railway bridge. Pass beneath the bridge and turn in along a track beside the farm, which is signed to Hell Gill Bridge.

After crossing the infant Ure at **How Beck Bridge**, keep left where the track splits and follow it gradually uphill. Meeting the High Way, go left to Hell Gill, some 200m further on.

The deep and spectacularly narrow chasm of **Hell Gill** is aptly named, and brings the source stream of the River Eden off the mountain above. Unfortunately, what would otherwise have been a dramatic spectacle is hidden from sight by fenced banks thick with trees overhanging each side, and the high parapet walls of the bridge. Anyone other than the exceptionally long-legged will need a bunk-up to peer over, but do not be too enthusiastic, for it is a seriously long and rocky way down. The wider scene across the valley, dominated by Swarth and Wild Boar fells, however, offers compensation, and is a view that now accompanies you for much of the walk.

The **High Way** is an ancient pack-horse route that connected Wensleydale with the Eden Valley, taking an elevated course to avoid the marshy terrain of the flat valley bottom balancing the watershed between the rivers Ure and Eden. It has been associated with Lady Anne Clifford since the middle of the 17th century, when she regularly travelled, until well into ripe old age (she died at 86), between her main seat at Skipton and her outlying properties in Westmorland.

Go back to the fork with the rising track and now take the left branch, which undulates easily across the hillside. The track soon twists across a stream, the fledgling River Ure, which has sprouted from the hillside some 250m higher up near the summit of Lunds Fell. Further on is **Washer Gill**, running through a secluded gorge. It is not as sensational as Hell Gill, but has the distinct advantage of being visible.

After turning in to cross the stream, the track winds back past the abandoned farmstead of **High Hall**, one of several along the hillside, and partly restored to preserve its character. Like many remote farms it doubled as an inn, deriving its business from the traders and drovers passing along the way. ◀ Further on, an elevated footbridge takes the path over **Lambfold Gill**, its necessity hinting at the ferocity with which the stream can surge down the hill. The deep cleft above the path is a stark contrast to the limestone through which the beck subsequently cleaves, highlighting the differing natures of the landscape fostered by the change of underlying rocks.

There is a credible story that Mary Queen of Scots rested here while she was being escorted from Carlisle to imprisonment at Bolton Castle in 1568.

Of interest is the rippling on many of the limestone boulders littering the gully, an effect of the chemical weathering caused by the slight acidity of rainwater.

Beyond, the track follows a line of shake holes across Keld Gill, and rises beside a clefted fault to the deserted farmstead of **High Dyke**, where it is crossed by a path that has come over Tarn Hill from Cotterdale.

Leave the High Way through a gate on the right, passing between the old pens and ruined buildings to the field behind. Bear right on a falling diagonal around the corner of a crumbling wall, aiming for a barn in the middle distance below a scarp of limestone. The way crosses a small and often dry gully, which just to the left debouches abruptly over a low cliff from which there is an unpretentiously spectacular view. ◀

Spared from the application of fertilisers and reseeding, these upland meadows harbour many wild flowers. In spring the violets, wood anemone, wild pansies and others break out from the green carpet and attract butterflies and bees.

Maintain your line down to the corner of a wall, and turn with it beside a deep gully embracing Keld Gill, to reach a ruined barn beside a stand of sycamore. Go right, crossing an intriguingly built bridge of layered slabs, supported on three high, drystone pillars, in whose joints sprout an amazing variety of ferns, mosses and small flowers.

Climb beyond to a gate and continue below the next barn, which also enjoyed the shade of a sycamore, although this one has been rent asunder, and both it and the barn have seen distinctly better days.

Lambfold Gill tumbles
in a waterfall at Shaws

The bouldery rocks are draped in the luxuriant green of mosses and ferns, and almost every crevice is burgeoning wild flowers.

Contour on across the hillside below the scar, re-crossing becks passed on the High Way that have breached the limestone cliff, as well as one or two more springing from lower down.

Reaching a signpost by a strip of wood, follow the wall around to the right to discover a wooden footbridge across **Lambfold Gill**, which here drops through an endearingly pretty gorge below a waterfall. ◄ The ongoing path climbs a flight of steps opposite to reach a gate, where a second waterfall is then revealed above.

Go left above the buildings of **Shaws** to another signpost and bear left again, descending to a gate in the bottom wall. Through that, swing right to a small gate, opening into a compact plantation of pine.

Breaking from the trees, head on across open ground towards a dilapidated barn. Even here, the rough pasture can be speckled with colour, marsh marigold and celandine erupting from the coarse tussock. Through a gate by the ruin, bear right to the corner of the upper wall. Cross a stream and climb to another gate.

Make your way through successive enclosures across the slope of the hill, heading for buildings set in a nest of trees, marked as **Low West End** on the map. Through a final gate a track winds down towards the farm.

After the first building, turn off right at a footpath sign to go between West End Farm House and the adjacent ruin. After crossing Lockshaw Gill, turn immediately left through a gate and head away by the right-hand wall. Beyond a fence stile bear left to a track, your outward route. Follow it left back to How Beck Bridge and keep left again back to the road at **Shaw Paddock**.

PART 5
NIDDERDALE

Idol rock seems to defy the laws of gravity (Walk 39)

WALK 39

Brimham Rocks

Start	Brimham Rocks (SE208645)
Distance	5¼ miles (8.4km)
Height gain	250m (820ft)
Time	2hr15
Terrain	Woodland and field paths
OS map	Explorer 298 – Nidderdale
Refreshments	Refreshment kiosk by Brimham House
Toilets	Adjacent to refreshment kiosk
Parking	National Trust car park (pay and display)

Exploring the rambling oak and birch woods below the escarpment of Brimham Moor, this is an outstandingly beautiful countryside walk, much of which follows the secluded valley of Fell Beck. The crowning highlight is, of course, the dramatic rockscape of Brimham itself, where the sculpted cliffs and outcrops of bare gritstone are amongst the most spectacular natural formations of their kind in the country.

Walk back from the car park along the main drive, abandoning it, as it bends to the road, for a track off right towards **Druid's Cave Farm**. Soon reaching a junction, go left and through a gate towards a farmhouse. There, swing left on a rough track, passing a barn and leaving through a gate onto a wooded hillside.

Bearing right, the ongoing path winds downhill within the fringe, later turning into the thick of the trees. Breaking out through a gate, bear left beside a fence to a stile and follow a clear path away to the right. Falling gently in and out of the cover, it eventually meets another track by **Low Wood House**. Go left, the way signed to Smelthouses.

Emerging onto a lane, walk uphill for some 50m to find a bridleway off on the right. This takes you through

The path through the woods from Smelthouses beside Fell Beck

more trees before dropping past a farm where you may see alpacas in the fields. As you pass the buildings, look for a path leaving through a gap in the right-hand wall, which winds around the edge of another small wood to join a drive beside a cottage, **Knox Hall**. Meeting a track at the bottom, go right, soon following a lively stream up a wooded valley to come back out onto the lane at **Smelthouses**.

Today, there is barely any visible evidence of the **lead smelting industry** that blackened this valley only a couple of centuries ago. Veins of lead ore outcrop on the nearby hills and may well have originally been exploited by the Romans. Large-scale mining was developed under the direction of the abbots of Furness and Byland abbeys, who built the first smelt mill here around 1445. They burned peat cut from Brimham Moor to fire the furnaces, which were used to extract the metal from the pounded rock. Production continued through the 18th and 19th centuries until the mines finally closed in 1896.

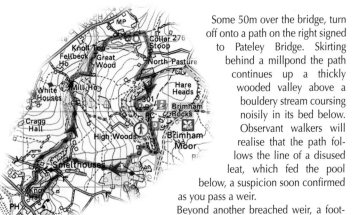

Some 50m over the bridge, turn off onto a path on the right signed to Pateley Bridge. Skirting behind a millpond the path continues up a thickly wooded valley above a bouldery stream coursing noisily in its bed below. Observant walkers will realise that the path follows the line of a disused leat, which fed the pool below, a suspicion soon confirmed as you pass a weir.

Beyond another breached weir, a footbridge takes the path to continue upstream on the other bank. Not far past the brick ruin of an engine

house, the path turns from the river below an abandoned quarry, climbing to meet a higher path. To the left, the way runs into lighter birch wood and then, bounded by fences, across an open glade. Once back in the trees, it meanders on to a junction.

The Dancing Bear is just one of Brimham's many fantastic rock features

Drop left to a bridge beside a ford, but rather than cross, mount a ladder stile on the right and follow a track at the edge of rising pasture. Towards the top of the field, look for a waymarked stile on the left. It is the first one you come to and heralds a path into more dense woodland. Leaving the trees behind, carry on beside a fence, but then, reaching a corner, swing left, dropping down a steep wooded bank to a confluence of streams.

Go right, crossing a stile and **Pencil Dike**, and continue up beside Black Dike at the edge of a rising grass bank. Reaching a hand gate, cross the stream and walk over a small meadow towards a farm. Pass left of the buildings to reach a track and follow it right past a little group of cottages.

Turning to grass, it climbs away to end through a gate into the corner of grazing. Strike right across a couple of fields towards **North Pasture Farm**. Emerging onto a track turn right, but where the track then swings in front of Flax Mill Cottage, keep ahead through a field gate. Through a gate at the far end, bear right and walk on across more fields to meet another track.

To the left, the path runs below a wooded bank, soon reaching the boundary of the National Trust's Brimham estate. There, double back on a path rising through the trees to emerge onto the more open heather and bilberry heath of **Brimham Moor**. Curving gently right, the main path shortly settles along the top of the rocky escarpment, taking you past some of the dramatic weatherworn outcrops for which the moor is famous.

Lesser paths split off in all directions in search of ever-more spectacular creations, inviting you to spend the remainder of the day in delightful exploration. The main path leads on to Brimham House, which was built in 1792 as a shooting lodge and now serves as a shop and visitor centre. To return to the parking areas, continue along the main drive past the toilets and refreshment kiosk.

BRIMHAM

The bedrock at Brimham was deposited some 320 million years ago, when the area lay in the delta of a great river that washed gritty sands from mountain regions far to the north. Rippling currents and slight differences in the sediments created cross-bedded planes of varying hardness, which, since laid bare by the last succession of ice ages, have been sculpted by the delicate erosion of wind-blown sand and winter freeze-thaw into fantastic shapes that defy the imagination and, in some cases, gravity too. Wander amongst the rocks and you will see their grotesque and surreal forms resolve into creatures, seemingly frozen into the landscape. It is little wonder that in the past they were imbued with supernatural forces and the place believed to be a Druid temple.

WALK 40

Ashfold Side

Start	Pateley Bridge (SE157654)
Distance	5½ miles (8.9km)
Height gain	250m (820ft)
Time	2hr15
Terrain	Tracks and field paths
OS map	Explorer 298 – Nidderdale
Refreshments	Choice of pubs and cafés in Pateley Bridge
Toilets	Opposite car park beside the bridge
Parking	Car park on B6265, south of bridge (pay and display)

Pateley Bridge is a renowned centre for ramblers, offering a huge choice of routes alongside the river and onto the wooded hills that rise at either side. This walk explores one of the tributary valleys, Ashfold Side, which was the scene of extensive mining operations during the 18th and 19th centuries. The substantial remains of the old Providence Mine provide an objective for the walk, which then returns across an open, verdant countryside where the hedgerows are thick with wild flowers in early summer.

Leaving the car park, walk towards the bridge, crossing the road to the start of a riverside footpath beside the public toilets. Elevated on a flood bank, it heads upstream past a recreation ground and a camping field. Ignore the bridge crossing the river and carry on along this bank at the edge of a large meadow.

Drawing level with a farm over to the left, the path forks. Cut across the grazing to meet a side-stream, here known as **Foster Beck**, and follow it up to a footbridge. Continue on the opposite bank, but then shortly leave the stream to emerge across a small field at a junction of lanes.

Take the one opposite, signed to Heathfield, soon branching off along a drive marked as a bridleway to

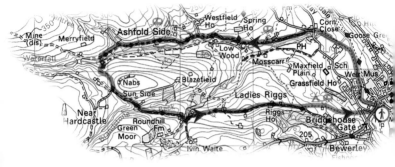

Heathfield Caravan Park. Occasional 'Nidderdale Way' signs keep you with the main through-track, past a succession of caravan and camping fields and occasional farms, but agreeable walking for all that.

Eventually, after a goodly mile (1.6km), the drive leaves the sites behind, degrading to a gravel track that continues into the less manicured countryside of the upper valley. The stream, now having changed its identity to **Ashfold Side Beck**, still runs below, bounding over a boulder-strewn bed.

Carry on, for a further ¾ mile (1.2km) along the narrowing valley, to a fork, where the Nidderdale Way is signed down to a footbridge over the stream below the **Providence** lead mines.

PROVIDENCE LEAD MINES

Veins of ore outcrop all around, and the whole of the upper valley has been mined for lead. Here, the steep slopes of the southern hillside are terraced with the spoil and debris from the Providence workings, whose deep and narrow shafts are still to be found on the hillside. Just downstream from the bridge are the remains of the water-powered engine houses and mill, where the ore was pounded and sorted in preparation for smelting. Rearing from a pit is a vertical drive shaft topped with a great, toothed crown wheel, now standing forlorn like some memorial totem.

The industry peaked in the 19th century, before the importation of cheaper Spanish lead forced a gradual decline on a home industry in which the best seams

A stark ruin above the mines

had in any case been largely worked out, and which could no longer compete economically. In its day, the valley would have been busy, noisy and thick with smoke, but now deserted and quiet, except for the babbling of the stream and the calls of birds, it portrays a sense of mournful abandonment.

The official footpath climbs left, right, and then left again up the hill, although any number of tracks weave up through the piles of bare dross spilling down the steep slope. Make for a prominent lone sycamore, past which the main track climbs south from the site.

At a junction beyond the crest, keep ahead, skirting the flank of a heather and bilberry hill richly speckled with tormentil, bird's-foot trefoil and other small flowers. On coming to a fork below another mine, keep right with the Nidderdale Way, which gently falls to a bridge across **Brandstone Beck**. Later, below Hill End, wind across a second stream to a junction and keep left.

The track, pleasingly fringed with wild flowers, undulates easily on across lush countryside. Walk on for a mile (1.6km) over Ladies Riggs, eventually reaching the corner of a large wood on the right where a waymarked path branches off beneath a clump of beech trees on the left. Over a stile, go right along the edge of open grazing, continuing beyond the field corner along an old, contained path, which falls towards the town.

Reaching a cottage, follow its drive down to emerge onto a back street at **Bridgehouse Gate** opposite the former Metcalfe Brewery. Go right and then left along a narrow ginnel, which cuts the corner to meet the main road. Pateley Bridge and the car park then lie just to the left.

WALK 41

Middlesmoor and
How Stean Gorge

Start	By Studfold Farm, Lofthouse (SE097733)
Distance	5¾ miles (9.3km)
Height gain	300m (984ft)
Time	2hr30
Terrain	Moorland tracks and field trods
OS map	Explorer 298 – Nidderdale
Refreshments	Pub at Middlesmoor, café at How Stean Gorge
Toilets	Beside the Crown Hotel in Middlesmoor
Parking	Lay-by on bend of main lane, just west of Lofthouse

The highlight of this walk is undoubtedly a visit to How Stean Gorge, a spectacular limestone ravine through which the river breaks out from its short valley to join the Nidd. But first, the route climbs along an ancient thoroughfare across the moor above Middlesmoor to gain a spectacular panorama across the upper reaches of Nidderdale.

From the car park, turn right to a junction and go ahead on the main lane to a bend. Pass through a kissing-gate in the left corner of the lay-by opposite and strike out to a gate partway along the end wall.

A trod develops at the edge of two more fields to reach a farm, Halfway House. Walk forward between the house and barn and then, faced with two gates, leave through the one on the left. Carry on up the hill towards **Middlesmoor**, emerging beside the churchyard entrance onto a cobbled back street. Bear left to the main street and turn up through the village past the Crown Hotel.

Leaving the village behind, the surface degrades to gravel and continues in steady ascent, signed to Scar House. Its widely spaced walls suggest an old drove

Unfortunately, the initially high walls exclude the wider vista opened up by the increasing height gain, although periodic field gates offer an opportunity for an appreciative pause.

road, along which the broad verges would have offered some grazing to the cattle herded through the hills to market. ◄

After 1½ miles (2.4km), and passing through a gate, the way crests the hill and begins a gradual, easy descent. Carry on for another ¼ mile (400m) or so to a bend, beyond which the ground suddenly falls more steeply to reveal a panorama into the upper reaches of Nidderdale.

On the other side of the valley, the high ground runs left from Dead Man's Hill over Little Whernside and on to Great Whernside, from whose flank is born the River Nidd. Below is the Scar House Reservoir, while the Angram Reservoir, which lies at the foot of Great Whernside, is hidden from view by the shoulder of the hill.

You can of course continue all the way down the hillside into the Nidd valley, meeting the service track just west of the dam, but you would then have to climb back to this point. So, rather than relinquish your hard-won height, retrace your steps to the gate, continuing for some 30m beyond to find another gate off on the right.

After briefly following the right-hand wall down, the line marked on the Ordnance Survey map wanders off to trace a parallel course some 100m to the left, occasionally marked by a waypost. The trod, however, remains largely discernible beside the wall, falling to meet a gravel track at the bottom.

Go left, passing over a cattle-grid into the next field. Again, the path marked off right on the map is hard to follow on the ground, and it is best to continue along the track to the next wall and then follow it right to find a step stile towards the bottom. Over that, cut the corner to a field gate on the right and then bear left towards **Intake Farm**. The path passes through a gate immediately to the right of the building.

Now in the lower pastures, the going improves. Keep ahead to a small gate, just left of an abandoned farmstead at the far side, **Ruscoe**. A few steps beyond the ruin, look for a waymarked gate in the right-hand wall. Bear left to pass through another gate below a barn and maintain your slanting descent down the field.

Over stiles, a path develops along the side of a narrow, wooded valley, How Stean Beck, gushing noisily below, although initially hidden by the trees. Steadily losing height, the way falls to the river, here flowing over slabs of bedrock and boulders, overhung by a delightful leafy canopy.

All too soon the path bursts from the trees to continue at the field edge, relinquishing its intimate contact with the river. Ignore gates back to the bank and carry on to a ladder stile. In the third field, a waymarked path joins through a gate from a bridge below across How Stean Beck.

Although the route does not go that way, it is worth wandering down to have a look, for by now the river has fallen into a deepening ravine, and gives a hint of what you will see if you visit How Stean Gorge itself.

Returning to the field, head up, cutting the corner to a gap stile partway along the right-hand wall. Through that, strike out across the next field to the lower of two gates interrupting the far wall. Keep going until you reach a gate beside a barn, through it, swinging right down to a second gate. Bear left across a final field, crossing a bridge to the entrance of **How Stean Gorge**.

Walk out to the lane and go left, following it down to swing over a bridge. Carry on to a road junction and keep ahead along the main lane back to the lay-by.

Water has sculpted the rock into extravagant shapes in How Stean Gorge

HOW STEAN GORGE

The 20m deep gorge was first opened up as an attraction for Victorian tourists, who, with the coming of the railway into the valley, were able to take advantage of cheap excursions to the countryside from the industrial towns surrounding Leeds. The place became known as 'Little Switzerland', and pathways and bridges were constructed to give access to the spectacular features of this otherwise inaccessible canyon, revealing wonders that remain just as marvellous today.

The gorge originally formed as a cave, the river dissolving its way through cracks in the limestone. In places the walls still bear traces of old stalactites and smooth flows created by the evaporation of lime-rich water in the closed confines, as well as deposits of coarser tufa, resulting from the deposition of lime in the open air after the roof of the cavern collapsed. The riverbed is intriguingly pocked with moulins – circular hollows and pits ground out by pebbles washed round and round by the flow of the stream. Elsewhere the rock has been quarried, exposing many fossils, and bearing marks where the rock was drilled for blasting.

A side-cavern, known as Tom Taylor's Cave, leads through to a pot, Cat Hole, at the back of the car park, and is said to have been the haunt of a local highwayman. In 1868, a local lad discovered a number of silver coins hidden there, which are thought to have been associated with the Roman lead mines at Greenhow.

The war memorial in Lofthouse

WALK 42
Nidderdale

Start	Lofthouse (SE101734)
Distance	7½ miles (12.1km)
Height gain	375m (1230ft)
Time	3hr
Terrain	Tracks and field trods
OS map	Explorer 298 – Nidderdale
Refreshments	Pubs in Lofthouse and Middlesmoor, café at How Stean Gorge
Toilets	Middlesmoor, beside the Crown Hotel
Parking	Car park in Lofthouse

Accessed only by a service lane to the upper dams and the handful of farms dotting the higher dale, the Nidd valley above Lofthouse is a quiet and beautiful place. This walk begins along a track, which served as the main thoroughfare before the reservoirs were built, returning across the hillside past the remote village of Middlesmoor. Amongst the interesting features encountered are the sinks and resurgences of the river, which here flows through a bed of limestone layered in the hills.

Head up through the village, winding past two commemorative drinking fountains. The first was erected in March 1920 as a war memorial, and offers the healthy advice: 'A pint of cold water three times a day is the surest way to keep doctor away', and 'If you want to be healthy, wealthy and stout, use plenty of cold water inside and out'. The second lies just around the corner, tucked away on the right, and celebrated the Armistice of 1918. Sadly both are now dry.

A short pull takes you out of the village, but as the lane then bends, branch off left along a grass track signed to Scar House Reservoir. **Thrope Lane**, the old route

into the higher valley before the construction of the reservoirs, undulates pleasantly along the hillside, and as it later breaks to more open ground, gives a splendid view along the valley.

A mile (1.6km) of enjoyable walking brings you to **Thrope Farm** and, if you wish, the opportunity to shorten the walk. However, there is still much of interest to see higher up the valley, and the main route continues beyond the farm along the Nidderdale Way through the gate ahead. Shortly falling, the track meets the riverbed, which for most of the year is dry, the water having gone to ground.

This part of the valley is studded with **sinks and pots** that lead to the cave system through which the river flows. Some of the more famous are marked on the map – Manchester Hole and Goyden Pot – but there are others too, even lying in the riverbed itself. You might spot the entrances – they are marked by round covers, intended to stop the unwary falling in, as well as to prevent the openings from becoming blocked by debris. However, all are extremely narrow and, unlike the nearby Stump Cross Caverns, definitely not for the inexperienced.

When the river is dry you can easily cross to a gate through which the path continues along the opposite

234

bank. The course of the river narrows to a gorge, where you might notice the entrance to a mine adit beside the path. Finally emerging into a field, follow waymarks to the second of two gates, which leads to an open yard area by **Limley Farm**.

Walk ahead between the buildings, dogging right and left at the far end of the farm around a final barn to re-cross the riverbed. Climb away beside a wall at the foot of a steep bank, higher up swinging right and then left to reach a gate into the garden of **Thwaite House**. Go beside the left wall to a barn and wind around the rear of it to emerge onto a gravel track.

Leading away, the track contours the hillside high above the river, soon curving around to reveal a lovely view into the upper reaches. In the distance is the Scar House Dam, impressively high in its own right, but from here further exaggerated by the depth of the intervening dale.

Across Nidderdale from Thrope Lane to Middlesmoor

The continuing track winds past **Bracken Ridge Farm**, its elevated course separating the moor above from the lusher pastures below. Carry on past occasional cottages for a further ¾ mile (1.2km) until you reach **New Houses Edge Farm**. There, drop from the track and double back around the end barn to a field gate behind the farmhouse.

Strike a slanting descent to a gate in the lower corner of the field and keep on above a grass bank towards a wood, where you will find a stile in its indented corner. Pass through the trees and walk on along the bottom edge of the field beyond to emerge through a gate at the far side onto a track. Follow it right, past cottages, down to a bridge across the Nidd.

However, immediately before the bridge, turn back sharp left along a short track into the field, because contrary to what might be shown on older editions of the Ordnance Survey map, the path from **New Houses** has been diverted beside the river.

Walk away above the bank, passing through a kissing-gate and eventually reaching a footbridge across the river, at this point full of water. Over that, bear left to cut a shallow bend in the river, and continue beyond a small copse across the next meadow.

A stile in the fence suggests the path once more crosses the Nidd (which at this point is usually dry), but in fact it merely provides access to **Manchester Hole**, tucked below the scar opposite. You can actually see into this one, the river running at its base, but although the entrance looks inviting, any slight rise in water levels can quickly cut off the escape, making it a very dangerous place for the inexperienced.

The way remains on the west bank, following the course of the river from field to field. Later on the valley narrows, the path following it through to emerge at **Limley Farm**. Pass between the barns to meet your outward route. Turning right, walk out through the farm and retrace your steps along the Nidderdale Way to **Thrope Farm**.

Rather than simply go back the way you came, you can extend the ramble up the hill via Middlesmoor and return by way of How Stean Gorge. Swing right through the farmyard, following its access track down to a bridge. Immediately over, cross the fence into the field on the left and follow the riverbank downstream.

Partway along, bear away to a gate opening in the middle of the end wall and continue the line to the top corner of the next field, there climbing out onto the lane, formerly the trackbed of the Nidderdale Railway.

NIDDERDALE RAILWAY

The quiet lane running into the upper valley from Lofthouse follows the course of the Nidderdale Railway, laid at the beginning of the 20th century to transport materials and equipment from the main railhead at Pateley Bridge for the construction of the Scar House Reservoir.

Scar House, the last of the three dams to be erected in Nidderdale, was constructed by Bradford Corporation rather than private contractors. They also operated the railway, the only municipal line in the country which, although classed as a light railway, was built to the standard gauge and carried passenger traffic as far as Lofthouse. It was a popular excursion for a time, but business declined and it was eventually closed to passengers in 1929. The track was taken up when work on the dam finished in 1936, 15 years after it had begun.

Go left to a stile, some 50m along on the right, and cut left across the corner to a second stile. Head away on an uphill diagonal towards distant **Middlesmoor**, crossing from field to field to a stand of conifers climbing the hill. Pass through and resume your former line, ultimately leaving the fields through a gate onto a track, which leads past St Chad's Church into the centre of the village.

If you are looking for refreshment, the Crown Hotel lies just up the hill, otherwise, turn left and follow the lane out of the village. After rounding a sharp left-hand bend, abandon the lane through a stile adjacent to a gate on the right.

Head down beside the boundary hedge, continuing until you reach a wall stile in the third field. Keep on this side of the wall and turn left, striking across the field to

The higher reaches of Nidderdale from Thwaite House

the lower of two gates in the far wall. Keep going across subsequent fields until you reach a gate beside a barn, swinging right through it down to a second gate. Bear left across a final field and over a bridge to reach the entrance of **How Stean Gorge**.

Joining the lane beyond the café, follow it down the hill, shortly bending with it across a bridge. Walk on to a road junction and keep ahead along the main lane to a bend, where there is a large lay-by.

Pass through the right-most of the two kissing-gates, wind around a farm shed and walk beside the village cricket square to reach the Scar House lane opposite the small fire station building. Cross to a path opposite, which leads to an old pack-horse bridge. On the far bank, the path swings right, rising into the village to emerge by the war memorial just up from the car park.

WALK 43

Little Whernside

Start	Scar House Reservoir (SE096766)
Distance	10 miles (16.1km)
Height gain	440m (1444ft)
Time	4hr
Terrain	Tracks and rough moorland trods
OS map	Explorer OL30 – Yorkshire Dales (Northern & Central Areas)
Refreshments	Farm teas during summer weekends at nearby High Woodale
Toilets	By car park
Parking	Car park by Scar House Reservoir

Despite its length and the vertical height gained, this is an easy and extremely satisfying walk given the right conditions, which typically would fall during a prolonged dry spell or on a settled and clear frosty day. Wet weather, however, can make the going very arduous across the marshy ground of the tops, and poor visibility will require some compass work, and renders the walk almost pointless, unless you are out purely for exercise.

From the far end of the car park, go right past the toilets and then left along the main drive. Rather than turn across the **Scar House Dam**, continue along the track above the southern bank of the reservoir, the way signed to Angram Dam.

There follows a pleasant 1½ mile (2.4km) walk up the valley. To the right, the ground rises to Dead Man's Hill, while ahead is the day's objective, Little Whernside. Eventually the valley turns to reveal the **Angram Dam**, smaller than Scar House but no less impressive.

Carried on an arched causeway, the track swings across the dam, giving a superb view to Great Whernside,

From the Angram Dam to the head of Scar House Reservoir

NIDDERDALE RESERVOIRS

The complex of Nidderdale reservoirs was built to provide Bradford with water. The later part of the 19th century had seen a phenomenal expansion of the town's textile industry, with a corresponding rise in population, and the town, in competition with others, was literally scouring the surrounding countryside in search of suitable supplies.

Upper Nidderdale was finally selected as being geologically sound, and with a large catchment and minimal resident population. Three dams were planned, the two upper ones to provide water supplies, while Gorthwaite was built as a compensation reservoir to maintain a consistent river flow through the lower valley, where many mills were still reliant on water.

In 1893, work began on the 31 mile (50km) aqueduct needed to transport the water to the town. A major obstacle was Greenhow Hill, necessitating a 6 mile (9.7km) tunnel, but the work was completed in 1901.

Angram was the first of the two upper dams to be built, started in 1903 and finished in 1919. The dam stretches 365m across the valley and is 40m high, giving the reservoir a capacity of 1042 million gallons (4737 million litres) of water.

Scar House Dam is 600m long, stands 71m above the valley floor and can hold more than twice as much water. It took 15 years to build and was opened in 1936.

which closes the head of the valley. Its flanks pucker into two main catchments feeding the lake, the one on the right, although springing from lower down the hill, being credited as the source of the River Nidd.

Emerging from the northern portals of the dam, immediately leave the track to find a grass path that heads back across the hillside above the lower reservoir. After dipping across Wench Gill, the distinct path continues across occasional stiles, eventually coming out onto a track. Follow it left through a gate to a junction, leaving just before it through a smaller gate on the left.

Marked as a bridleway, a faint but persistent trod strikes an easy slant up the hill. As it later closes with the wall to the right, watch out for the path passing through a gap. It continues above the opposite flank, cutting the corner to pass through another break a little further on. The path carries on unvaryingly across the open moor, gradually gaining height along the valley side.

You will eventually come to a wall, which climbs direct to the summit, only ½ mile (500m) away. Although an indistinct path beside it beckons, the easier, if more roundabout route continues with the trod through the gate.

Apart from negotiating occasional boggy streams draining the hags above, the going is generally good and the way remains clear. After later crossing a second wall, the path makes a beeline for the shallow, sweeping saddle that connects Little Whernside with its more substantial relative.

The **watershed** is marked by a long boundary running the full length of the ridge, the ground beyond falling into the higher reaches of Coverdale, and despite the modest slopes on either side, there is a wonderful view.

Follow the wall to the right, the path at first quite boggy until it climbs above the saddle. For a time the going improves, but higher up the way passes into an extensive peat hag, much eroded to create a wild landscape. Distant views disappear as you pick the best way through, but with the accompanying fence as a guide, there is no danger of wandering off course.

A delicate drystone arch once carried the wall across the beck above Scar House Reservoir

Eventually passing through a gated fence, the continuation of the wall encountered on the way up, the path broaches the summit plateau of **Little Whernside**, the high point marked a little further on by a small pile of stones on the opposite side of the fence.

The hags bristle with heather, and the depressions are softened with patches of cottongrass, but the flatness blocks off the distant views and it is a lonely place, the silence broken only by the calls of moorland birds or, occasionally, the more intrusive roar of a combat plane on exercise.

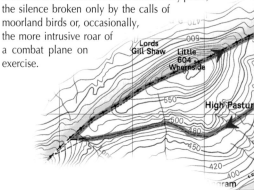

Walk on beside the fence. When, after some ten minutes, the ground begins to fall more noticeably out of the peat, the view suddenly opens ahead, revealing on the one hand the full length of Coverdale, while on the other is the upper reach of Nidderdale.

Levelling to another saddle, the ground is again predictably boggy in places, the fence leading you eventually to a gate through which a track rises from Coverdale. To the right, it falls gently towards Nidderdale and gives a splendid view back to Little Whernside, from here its platform top suggestive of some archaic temple or fort.

The sense of upland remoteness is a striking contrast to the lush meadows and rich woodlands cupped in the lower valley. Firm ground encourages a sprightly step, and the way soon fragments to fall more steeply off the hill, in due course bringing you back to the junction above Scar House Reservoir encountered on the way out.

You can, of course, go back the way you came, but an alternative lies along the track to the left, soon passing a clump of trees sheltering the ruin of one of the many steadings that dotted the upper valley before it was flooded beneath the reservoirs.

Beyond there is a grand view to the Scar House Dam, and on the opposite side of the valley a steep incline rises above the car park to quarries from which stone was cut for the dam's construction. At the foot of the lake, bear right, dropping to the main drive, which takes you across the dam and back to the car park.

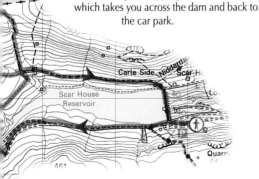

SCAR HOUSE VILLAGE

The curious terraces that line the road near the car park are all that remain of Scar House village, built to house the dam construction workers. Up to 1250 people lived here, many of them Irish navvies who were accommodated in well-furnished hostels, while families had bungalows with the luxury of running water and inside toilets. There was a cinema, dance hall, recreation and sports facilities, and a small hospital, as well as a canteen, shops, bank, post office and chapel. The standards far exceeded those under which most people of the day lived, and many of its temporary residents had fond memories of the place long after the work had finished and they dispersed across the country to other jobs.

APPENDIX A

Route summaries and suggestions for longer routes

Walk	Page	Title	Start	Grid	Distance mile/km	Height gain m/ft	Time	OS Map
1	45	Sedbergh and the River Rawthey	Sedbergh	SD657921	5/8	145/476	2hr	OL19
2	49	The Rivers Rawthey and Lune from Sedbergh	Sedbergh	SD657921	6½/10.5	215/705	2hr30	OL19
3	54	Winder, Calders and the Calf	Sedbergh	SD657921	9¾/15.7	855/2805	4hr45	OL19
4	59	Carlin Gill and Fell Head from Fairmile Gate	Fairmile Gate	SD629977	6¼/10.1	570/1870	3hr	OL19
5	64	The Rawthey from the Cross Keys Inn	The Cross Keys	SD698969	5/8	170/558	2hr	OL19
6	67	Cautley Crag and the Calf	The Cross Keys	SD698969	7/11.3	640/2100	3hr15	OL19
7	71	Around Wandale Hill	Rawthey Bridge	SD712979	6/9.7	320/1050	2hr30	OL19
8	75	The River Rawthey's higher reaches	Rawthey Bridge	SD712979	5/8	260/853	2hr	OL19
9	79	Grisedale	Garsdale Head	SD786919	5/8	275/902	2hr	OL19

Walk	Page	Title	Start	Grid	Distance mile/km	Height gain m/ft	Time	OS Map
10	84	High Seat	B6270, Lamps Moss	SD808042	4¼/6.8	215/705	2hr30	OL19
11	87	Pendragon Castle and Little Fell	Pendragon Castle	NY782026	6/9.7	395/1296	2hr30	OL19
12	92	Wild Boar Fell and Swarth Fell	Cotegill Bridge, Aisgill	SD773969	8/12.9	535/1755	3hr30	OL19
13	100	Apedale and Harkerside Moor	Grinton, Redmire road	SE038963	9¾/15.7	440/1444	4hr	OL30
14	105	Grinton and Maiden Castle	Grinton	SE046984	4¾/7.6	210/689	2hr	OL30
15	109	Fremington Edge	Reeth	SE038992	7¼/11.7	415/1362	3h	OL30
16	114	Slei Gill	Langthwaite	NZ005023	5¾/9.3	320/1050	2hr30	OL30
17	118	Whaw to Dale Head	Whaw Bridge	NY980042	4½/7.2	220/722	2hr	OL30
18	121	Old Gang and Surrender	Surrender Bridge	SD989998	5½/8.9	265/869	2hr15	OL30
19	126	Beside the River Swale from Gunnerside	Gunnerside	SD950982	4½/7.2	175/574	1hr45	OL30
20	130	Gunnerside Gill	Gunnerside	SD950982	7/11.3	480/1575	3hr	OL30
21	135	Ivelet Bridge from Muker	Muker	SD910978	5/8	250/820	2hr	OL30
22	138	Great Shunner Fell and Lovely Seat from Thwaite	Thwaite	SD892980	9½/15.3	780/2559	4hr30	OL30

Walk	Page	Title	Start	Grid	Distance mile/km	Height gain m/ft	Time	OS Map
23	142	Muker, Thwaite and Kisdon Force from Keld	Keld	NY892012	8¼/13.3	485/1591	3hr30	OL30
24	148	Whitsundale and the head of the River Swale	Keld	NY892012	8/12.9	365/1197	3hr15	OL30
25	153	A walk in Coverdale	Carlton	SE069847	6½/10.5	260/853	2hr30	OL30
26	159	West Witton and the River Ure to Redmire Force	West Witton	SE067884	5½/8.9	140/459	2hr	OL30
27	163	Aysgarth to West Burton	Aysgarth	SE011884	4½/7.2	175/574	1hr45	OL30
28	168	Aysgarth Falls	Aysgarth	SE011884	4/6.4	130/426	1hr30	OL30
29	172	Ivy Scar From Aysgarth	Aysgarth	SE011887	7/11.3	210/689	2hr30	OL30
30	176	Whitfield Gill Force and Mill Gill Falls	Askrigg	SD947910	3¼/5.2	200/656	1hr30	OL30
31	180	The Wensleydale railway and River Ure stepping-stones	Bainbridge	SD934901	3½/5.6	80/262	1hr15	OL30
32	184	The Wensleydale railway and Skell Gill	Bainbridge	SD934901	5½/8.9	175/574	2hr	OL30
33	188	Bainbridge to Semer Water	Bainbridge	SD934901	5½/8.9	300/984	2hr15	OL30
34	193	Aysgill Force	Hawes	SD875898	4¼/6.8	150/492	1hr45	OL2 or OL30

Walk	Page	Title	Start	Grid	Distance mile/km	Height gain m/ft	Time	OS Map
35	196	Dodd Fell Hill and Drumaldrace	Hawes	SD875898	11½/18.5	570/1870	4hr45	OL2
36	203	Cotterdale	Hardraw	SD866911	7/11.3	360/1181	3hr	OL19
37	207	Great Shunner Fell from Hardraw	Hardraw	SD866911	10½/16.9	555/1821	4hr15	OL19
38	212	The High Way	B6259, Shaw Paddock	SD784952	5¼/8.4	205/673	2hr	OL19
39	218	Brimham Rocks	Brimham Rocks	SE208645	5¼/8.4	250/820	2hr15	EXP 298
40	223	Ashfold Side	Pateley Bridge	SE157654	5½/8.9	250/820	2hr15	EXP 298
41	227	Middlesmoor and How Stean Gorge	Lofthouse	SE097733	5¾/9.3	300/984	2hr30	EXP 298
42	233	Nidderdale	Lofthouse	SE101734	7½/12.1	375/1230	3hr	EXP 298
43	239	Little Whernside	Scar House Reservoir	SE069766	10/16.1	440/1444	4hr	OL30

Walk	Page	Title	Start	Grid	Distance mile/km	Height gain m/ft	Time	OS Map
Extended Walks								
1,2	45/49	The Rivers Rawthey and Lune from Sedbergh	Sedbergh	SD657921	10/16.1	320/1050	3hr45	OL19
11,12	87/92	Mallerstang's western ridge	Pendragon Castle	NY782026	13¾/22.1	865/2838	6hr	OL19
15,16	109/114	Fremington Edge and Slei Gill	Reeth or Langthwaite	SE038992 or NZ005023	12½/20.1	760/2493	5hr30	OL30
19,20	126/130	Gunnerside Gill and the River Swale	Gunnerside	SD950982	11½/18.5	655/2149	4hr45	OL30
23,21	142/135	Keld to Ivelet Bridge	Keld	NY892012	11½/18.5	595/1952	5hr	OL30
23,24	142/148	Muker to the head of the River Swale	Muker	SD910978	15½/24.9	785/2575	6hr30	OL30
26,28	159/168	Redmire Force and Aysgarth Falls	West Witton	SE067884	11/17.7	370/1213	4hr15	OL30
27,28	163/168	West Burton and Aysgarth Falls	Aysgarth	SE011884	6½/10.5	255/837	2hr30	OL30
31,33	180/188	From the River Ure to Bainbridge	Bainbridge	SD934901	7¼/11.7	330/1083	3hr	OL30
41,42	227/233	Upper Nidderdale and How Stean Gorge	Lofthouse	SE101734	11¼/18.1	575/1886	4hr30	EXP 298

APPENDIX B
Where to find out more

National Park Information
Yorkshire Dales National Park Authority
www.yorkshiredales.org.uk
Tel: 0300 456 0030
Offices:
Yoredale, Bainbridge, Leyburn, North Yorkshire DL8 3EL
Tel 01969 652300
Colvend, Grassington, Skipton, North Yorkshire BD23 5LB
Tel 01756 751600

National Park Information Centres
Aysgarth Falls, tel 01969 662910
Grassington, tel 01756 751690
Hawes, tel 01969 666210
Malham, tel 01729 833200
Reeth, tel 01748 884059

Rights of Way Issues
Yorkshire Dales National Park, tel 0300 456 0030
North Yorkshire County Council, contact via www.northyorks.gov.uk
Cumbria County Council, tel 01228 606060

Public Transport
Dales Bus
www.dalesbus.org
Traveline, tel 0871 200 22 33;
www.traveline.info

Tourist Information
Dry Sand Foundry, Foundry Square, Holbeck, Leeds LS11 5DL
www.yorkshire.com

Local Tourist Information Offices
(*Seasonal opening)

Hawes ,tel: 01969 666210;
hawes@ytbtic.co.uk

Kirkby Stephen, tel 01768 371199;
visit@uecp.org.uk

Leyburn, tel 01989 623814;
info@welcometoleyburn.co.uk

Pateley Bridge*, tel 01423 714953;
pbtic@harrogate.gov.uk

Reeth, tel 01748 884 059;
reeth@yorkshiredales.org.uk

Richmond, tel 01609 532980;
ric@richmond.org

Sedbergh, tel 015396 20125;
tic@sedbergh.org.uk

Other Useful Organisations
National Trust
www.nationaltrust.org.uk
Membership and general enquiries:
PO Box 574, Manvers, Rotherham S63 3FH
Tel 0344 800 1895

Regional office:
Goddards, 27 Tadcaster Road, Dringhouses,
York YO24 1GG
Tel 01904 702021
yne.customerenquiries@nationaltrust.org.uk

Youth Hostels Association
(Head office) Trevelyan House, Dimple Road, Matlock, Derbyshire DE4 3YH
www.yha.org.uk
Customer services and reservations: tel 0800 019 1700 or 01629 592700;
customerservices@yha.org.uk

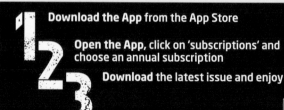

LISTING OF CICERONE GUIDES

SCOTLAND

Backpacker's Britain: Northern Scotland
Ben Nevis and Glen Coe
Cycle Touring in Northern Scotland
Cycling in the Hebrides
Great Mountain Days in Scotland
Mountain Biking in Southern and Central Scotland
Mountain Biking in West and North West Scotland
Not the West Highland Way
Scotland
Scotland's Best Small Mountains
Scotland's Mountain Ridges
Skye's Cuillin Ridge Traverse
The Ayrshire and Arran Coastal Paths
The Border Country
The Borders Abbeys Way
The Cape Wrath Trail
The Great Glen Way
The Great Glen Way Map Booklet
The Hebridean Way
The Hebrides
The Isle of Mull
The Isle of Skye
The Skye Trail
The Southern Upland Way
The Speyside Way
The Speyside Way Map Booklet
The West Highland Way
The West Highland Way Map Booklet
Walking Highland Perthshire
Walking in Scotland's Far North
Walking in the Angus Glens
Walking in the Cairngorms
Walking in the Ochils, Campsie Fells and Lomond Hills
Walking in the Pentland Hills
Walking in the Scottish Borders
Walking in the Southern Uplands
Walking in Torridon
Walking Loch Lomond and the Trossachs
Walking on Arran
Walking on Harris and Lewis
Walking on Jura, Islay and Colonsay
Walking on Rum and the Small Isles
Walking on the Orkney and Shetland Isles
Walking on Uist and Barra
Walking the Cape Wrath Trail
Walking the Corbetts
Vol 1 South of the Great Glen
Walking the Corbetts
Vol 2 North of the Great Glen
Walking the Galloway Hills
Walking the Munros Vol 1 – Southern, Central and Western Highlands
Walking the Munros Vol 2 – Northern Highlands and the Cairngorms
Winter Climbs Ben Nevis and Glen Coe

Winter Climbs in the Cairngorms

NORTHERN ENGLAND TRAILS

Hadrian's Wall Path
Hadrian's Wall Path Map Booklet
The Coast to Coast Walk
The Coast to Coast Map Booklet
The Dales Way
The Dales Way Map Booklet
The Pennine Way
The Pennine Way Map Booklet

LAKE DISTRICT

Cycling in the Lake District
Great Mountain Days in the Lake District
Lake District Winter Climbs
Lake District: High Level and Fell Walks
Lake District: Low Level and Lake Walks
Mountain Biking in the Lake District
Outdoor Adventures with Children – Lake District
Scrambles in the Lake District – North
Scrambles in the Lake District – South
Scrambles in the Lake District – South and East
Short Walks in Lakeland Book 2: North Lakeland
The Cumbria Way
Trail and Fell Running in the Lake District
Walking the Lake District Fells – Buttermere
Walking the Lake District Fells – Keswick
Walking the Lake District Fells – Langdale
Walking the Lake District Fells – Mardale and the Far East
Walking the Lake District Fells – Patterdale
Walking the Lake District Fells – Wasdale

NORTH WEST ENGLAND AND THE ISLE OF MAN

Cycling the Pennine Bridleway
Cycling the Way of the Roses
Hadrian's Cycleway
Isle of Man Coastal Path
The Lancashire Cycleway
The Lune Valley and Howgills
The Ribble Way
Walking in Cumbria's Eden Valley
Walking in Lancashire
Walking in the Forest of Bowland and Pendle
Walking on the Isle of Man
Walking on the West Pennine Moors
Walks in Silverdale and Arnside

NORTH EAST ENGLAND, YORKSHIRE DALES AND PENNINES

Cycling in the Yorkshire Dales
Great Mountain Days in the Pennines
Mountain Biking in the Yorkshire Dales
St Oswald's Way and St Cuthbert's Way
The Cleveland Way and the Yorkshire Wolds Way
The Cleveland Way Map Booklet
The North York Moors
The Reivers Way
The Teesdale Way
Trail and Fell Running in the Yorkshire Dales
Walking in County Durham
Walking in Northumberland
Walking in the North Pennines
Walking in the Yorkshire Dales: North and East
Walking in the Yorkshire Dales: South and West

WALES AND WELSH BORDERS

Cycle Touring in Wales
Cycling Lon Las Cymru
Glyndwr's Way
Great Mountain Days in Snowdonia
Hillwalking in Shropshire
Hillwalking in Wales – Vols 1&2
Mountain Walking in Snowdonia
Offa's Dyke Path
Offa's Dyke Map Booklet
Ridges of Snowdonia
Scrambles in Snowdonia
Snowdonia: 30 Low-level and easy walks – North
Snowdonia: 30 Low-level and easy walks – South
The Cambrian Way
The Ceredigion and Snowdonia Coast Paths
The Pembrokeshire Coast Path
The Pembrokeshire Coast Path Map Booklet
The Severn Way
The Snowdonia Way
The Wales Coast Path
The Wye Valley Walk
Walking in Carmarthenshire
Walking in Pembrokeshire
Walking in the Forest of Dean
Walking in the Wye Valley
Walking on the Brecon Beacons
Walking on the Gower
Walking the Shropshire Way

DERBYSHIRE, PEAK DISTRICT AND MIDLANDS

Cycling in the Peak District
Dark Peak Walks
Scrambles in the Dark Peak

For full information on all our guides,
books and eBooks,
visit our website:
www.cicerone.co.uk

Explore the world with Cicerone

**walking • trekking • mountaineering • climbing • mountain biking •
cycling • via ferratas • scrambling • trail running • skills and techniques**

For over 50 years, Cicerone have built up an outstanding collection of
nearly 400 guides, inspiring all sorts of amazing experiences.

www.cicerone.co.uk – where adventures begin

- Our **website** is a treasure-trove for every outdoor adventurer. You
  can buy books or read inspiring articles and trip reports, get technical
  advice, check for updates, and view videos, photographs and mapping
  for routes and treks.

- **Register this book** or any other Cicerone guide in your member's
  library on our website and you can choose to automatically access
  updates and GPX files for your books, if available.

- Our **fortnightly newsletters** will update you on new publications and
  articles and keep you informed of other news and events. You can also
  follow us on Facebook, Twitter and Instagram.

We hope you have enjoyed using this guidebook. If you have any
comments you would like to share, please contact us using the form on
our website or via email, so that we can provide the best experience for
future customers.

CICERONE

Juniper House, Murley Moss Business Village, Oxenholme Road, Kendal LA9 7RL

✉ info@cicerone.co.uk   cicerone.co.uk